TL;DR: FINANCIAL LITERACY FOR EMPLOYEES OF COLORADO PUBLIC SCHOOLS

Optimizing Financial Decisions Based on your PERA and School District Benefits

Karl Fisch

ISBN-13: 979-8589787733

Library of Congress Control Number: 2018675309
Printed in the United States of America

CONTENTS

TL;DR: internet abbreviation for "too long, didn't read", meaning a post, article, or anything with words was too long, and whoever used the phrase didn't read it for that reason. (source: Urban Dictionary). (Each section of this book will include a brief TL;DR summary at the beginning of the section.)

"Luck is what happens when preparation meets opportunity." -Seneca

Visit **fischlearning.com/tldr** for links to websites, blogs, books, spreadsheets and other resources to learn more about all the topics covered in this book. If you have questions or feedback, or simply want to talk about your financial situation, please reach out to me at **karl@fischlearning.com**

For Jill
The best teacher I've ever met.
And my best friend.

Other Books by Karl
Find the entire TL;DR: Financial Literacy Series
at **http://bit.ly/fischtldr**

How This Book Is Organized

This book is divided into four major sections.

Part 1: Financial Literacy Basics for Everyone

Part 1 covers the information about financial literacy that is applicable to everyone, not just Colorado PERA members. Note that this part stands on its own and does not assume you are a PERA member.

Part 2: Your PERA Benefits

Part 2 focuses on your PERA benefits, and how they - along with the other benefits from your school district - impact almost all of the issues discussed in Part 1.

Part 3: How to Optimize Your Financial Planning to Take Advantage of PERA Benefits

Part 3 focuses on how you can optimize the decisions described in Part 1 based on the PERA benefits described in Part 2.

Part 4: Scenario Planning

Part 4 looks at several different "life scenarios" for PERA members as examples of how you might combine Parts 1, 2 and 3 into a coherent life financial plan. It includes links to detailed scenarios and spreadsheets.

Conclusion

Some closing thoughts, a request for feedback, and links to further resources.

Important: Both tax laws (frequently) and PERA benefit rules (occasionally) can change over time. As they change after publication of this book, I will do my best to keep the book updated. If you purchased the digital version, I will update it at Amazon and you can download the new version. If you purchased the print edition - or if you don't want to reread the entire digital version just to see what's changed - I will summarize the updates at **fischlearning.com/tldr**.

PART 1: FINANCIAL LITERACY BASICS FOR EVERYONE

Part 1 covers the information about financial literacy that is applicable to everyone, not just Colorado PERA members. Note that this part stands on its own and does not assume you are a PERA member.

1.1: INTRO & PURPOSE

TL;DR: Finances are such a huge part of your life that you should take the time to thoroughly educate yourself. Since many folks won't do that, this book is an attempt to quickly give you the basics. Many Colorado educators are also unaware of the fantastic advantages their PERA benefits give them and how they should impact all of their other financial decisions.

You shouldn't read this book. Really, you shouldn't. It's not that it's a bad book, it's just that it's an overly simplified look at finances and the decisions everyone should make to have a secure life financially. There are so many really good and much more in-depth resources that are readily available, both in books and on websites, that you should take advantage of those and give yourself the financial education you deserve. It wouldn't take a huge amount of time, I'd say somewhere between twenty and thirty hours to get a good grounding, and maybe between fifty and one hundred to be very well versed in almost everything you need to know. That may sound like a lot, but in comparison to the over 700,000 hours (and maybe many more) you are likely to be alive, it's a very small investment (pun intended). And since finances are such a huge part of your life, and of living your life the way you want to live it, it's worth the time investment. Compared to the over 14,000 hours you likely spent learning in K-12 schools (plus any post-secondary education), isn't it worth twenty to one hundred more to educate yourself in order to make good financial decisions?

"How long are you going to wait before you demand

the best for yourself?" – Epictetus

But many folks won't. There are a variety of reasons people don't invest the time to learn about finances.

- I'm really busy and it would take too long

- I wouldn't understand it anyway (I'm not smart enough/I'm not good at math)

- It doesn't matter because I don't make that much money and financial planning is for rich people

- The culture (at least in the United States) is that we don't talk about money and our finances

Or you may have a completely different reason. Whatever the reason, most people I know tend to move through their financial lives day by day, week by week, month by month, paycheck by paycheck. It's not that they don't try to make good financial decisions, or that they never plan ahead financially, it's that they don't take the time and make the effort to make a **coherent plan** for how they want to lead their financial lives. And they don't realize how simple most of the financial decisions they need to make are, and how easy it is to make good ones.

So this book is for those folks; for those people who won't take twenty (or thirty or fifty or one hundred) hours to really educate themselves, but can convince themselves to take one or two hours. By necessity, this will be a simplified look at finances and financial decisions for Colorado educators who are PERA members. (Most Colorado educators are not fully aware of their PERA benefits and how that should impact almost all of their other financial decisions throughout their adult lives.) I won't thoroughly explain topics. I won't discuss and link to the research that backs up the assertions. I won't have a lot of charts and tables, personal vignettes, or worksheets for you to complete. I will simply give advice that will be appropriate to about 90% of people about 90%

3

of the time. (I completely made those percentages up, but I'd say they are likely within ±5%.)

Most of the financial decisions we need to make in our lives are really relatively straightforward, and it doesn't take much more than an hour or two to go over them in a (superficial) fashion. Personal Finance is just that, it's "personal", so no book or website is going to be able to give you everything you need to know that is perfect for your individual circumstances. The hope is that perhaps, after reading this book (if you do), you will have the interest and the confidence to perhaps invest a few more hours to more thoroughly educate yourself, and to fill in the gaps in your "personal" situation that this book didn't adequately address. I could say a lot more but, well, that would kind of defeat the whole purpose of this book. If this book ends up too long and you don't read it, then I've failed (hence, the TL;DR).

Before we go any further, a disclosure. I am not a financial planner. I have no formal training in personal finance or investing, and no certifications. I am simply a lifelong learner, constantly curious, and have been interested in personal finance since working in a credit union during high school and college. I have continued to learn about finances my entire adult life and have frequently served as a resource for friends, family and colleagues. I somehow became the "go to" guy in my high school for other educators who had questions about school district benefits, PERA, and just finances in general. Partially as a result of that experience, I see the necessity for a book such as this, so I wanted to do my part to try to help Colorado educators become financially literate and optimize their financial lives based on their PERA benefits. While it would be nice to make a little bit of money from this, that's not really my expectation or my goal. This is a passion project for me. I hope you find it helpful.

So, about 100 pages. About an hour or two. Let's get started.

1.2: PHILOSOPHY & LIVING THE GOOD LIFE

TL;DR: *Financial planning should enable you to live the life you want to live.*

I almost left this section out, because it's more "explanation" and we're trying to avoid that and just get to the nitty gritty details (and hope that you will continue your education to learn more). But, in the end, I decided it was important to devote at least a short section to the purpose of financial planning (or at least my take on it). It provides a needed conceptual framework for how to think about the decisions discussed in the rest of the book, so bear with me for a few paragraphs.

Some people view financial planning as a way to get rich, others as a way to get by, and still others as a way to not just get by, but to be "secure" - whatever that means to them. Here is how I view financial planning: it's a necessary and critical part of living the good life. What's a "good life"? I don't know, everyone's definition is different. What's important is that you take the time to define what a good life is for you, and then **align your financial decisions with your values**.

> *"First say to yourself what you would be; and then do what you have to do." – Epictetus*

All the "conventional wisdom", all the "rules of thumb" that are talked about in financial circles (and I will include a few myself), assume that your vision of a good life is the same as whomever is telling you about the rule of thumb. While sometimes that will be a good fit, often it won't, and that's why it's really important to define what a "good life" looks like to you before embarking on this process. The key is making your own decisions in such a way that you are most likely to attain your version of the good life. The goal of this book is to help you plan your finances in such a way that you have the independence to lead the life you want to live; to give you as much control as possible over your financial situation so that your finances don't prevent you from living the life you want.

It's really that simple.

1.3: BASIC EQUATION: INCOME - EXPENSES = SAVINGS + INVESTMENTS

TL;DR: Make a budget if you wish, but it's more helpful to proactively focus on the four components of the equation.

I love math. I taught teenagers mathematics for my entire adult life. But I'm going to try to keep the math in this book to a minimum. It's not that I think you can't understand it (people aren't "bad" at math, they were often just bad at doing math class in school), it's that it's too easy to get distracted by the math (and miss the forest for the trees). But there's one basic equation that is important enough to include:

Income - Expenses = Savings + Investments

That equation really defines the parameters for every financial discussion/decision in this book. You start with your income, how much you make from your job(s) and any other sources of income you might have. Then you subtract off your expenses, what you spend. Whatever is left (and it's critical that there is something left) you can then decide to divide up between savings (money you might need in the relatively short term) and investments (money you won't need in the short term and therefore want to invest so that it will grow over time).

This is typically the point in a financial book where it would talk about the importance of a budget. I'm not going to do that. If you want to learn more about budgets, there are lots of books and websites that will help you and, for some folks, that might even be helpful. But in my experience, focusing on making a budget is an approach that isn't very helpful for most people. The way most people make budgets is **reactive**, they let their current circumstances define their budget and then point to the realities of the budget as the reason they can't get ahead. For most people, I think it's more helpful to be **proactive**, to recognize the realities (you do have to eat) but to design the life you want to lead instead of being restricted by the "assumed" realities of your current circumstances.

So, we're not going to specifically work on a budget in this book. Instead, we'll focus on the four components of that equation: **Income**, **expenses**, **savings**, and **investments**.

Income is how much you make, typically from your job(s), but some people have other sources of income as well. Obviously the larger your income is, the more money you have to work with, so if you have some ways to increase that income without negatively affecting your lifestyle (the good life, however you define that), do that. This can include doing things at your current job to increase your income, like taking on more responsibility, working more hours or a different shift, or increasing your skills in a way that makes you more valuable. It could also include other ways of making income, often referred to as "side hustles", things you do outside your regular job to earn extra income. It's really important if you decide to take on any side hustles that you only take on those that provide some extra income but don't negatively affect the life you want to live.

> *"What difference does it make, after all, what your position in life is if you dislike it yourself?"* – Seneca

And, ultimately, it will be **passive income**, income you make from your investments, that will allow you to retire.

Expenses is what you spend your money on, and this is the component that you typically have the most control over (see the next chapter). This will require the most thinking and work on your part to align your expenses with the life you want to live.

Savings is the money you have set aside for possible short-term use. It's money that you don't need to live on day-to-day or week-to-week, but that is available either for some expense you know is coming up (maybe holiday presents you are planning on buying, or perhaps you know you will be buying a new computer in the next year), or as a "rainy day" fund for an unexpected expense (your water heater needs service).

Investments is the money you have set aside for the long-term and, next to expenses, is the component you will want to do the most thinking about. Some people have trouble distinguishing between savings and investments, it's really the factor of time and purpose that distinguish them. Savings are short-term and their purpose is much more limited. Investments are long-term, we're going to say money you don't plan on spending for at least five years (and hopefully many more) and the purpose is typically (although not always) broader.

So, that's enough explanation, let's dive in.

1.4: SPENDING & SAVING

TL; DR: Your savings rate is more important than how much you earn on investments. And since your spending determines your savings rate, your spending rate is key.

"Curb your desire—don't set your heart on so many things and you will get what you need." – Epictetus

A lot of people spend a lot of time talking about how to make a lot of money in the stock market. I'll certainly spend a little time later in this book on the topic of investments as well. But a key point to remember is that you can't control what the market returns, the market is going to do its thing no matter what you do. What you can control is how much you save and therefore how much you invest. Your savings rate is much more important than trying to beat the market with your investments.

And here's the thing, your savings rate is really just a reflection of your spending. While there are certainly things you can do to increase your income, on a day-to-day basis most people have much more discretion over what they spend than over what they make. So your savings rate is pretty much going to be determined by your spending; spend less, save more (and then invest more). (See **bit.ly/spendingmatters** and **bit.ly/tldrpenny** for more.)

There have been entire books written about this, but this is the Karl's Notes version (sorry Cliff and Spark):

- In general, spending on "things" doesn't bring you happiness. Spending on experiences that are meaningful to you is more likely to increase your happiness.

- Human beings adjust quickly to new circumstances. In terms of spending, this is often referred to as the "**hedonic treadmill**". When you buy something new, you experience pleasure for a little while, then you get used to it and you need to buy something else to get a new fix. As your income (hopefully) increases over time, so does your lifestyle, so things that used to be "luxuries" are now considered necessities, and you begin inflating your lifestyle to match your new earnings (this is often referred to as "**lifestyle creep**"). Once you get on this "hedonic treadmill", it's hard to get off.

- "Keeping up with the Joneses" is a cliche, but it's a cliche that is based in truth. The problem is that your neighbors' (or friends', or family's) spending is visible, but their savings isn't. When your next door neighbor gets a new car, you'll probably see it. When your next door neighbor contributes more to their 401k, you probably won't.

- "**Opportunity Cost**" is an economic term, but it's pretty easy to understand. If you spend money (or time) on one thing, you don't have that money (or time) available to spend on something else. Every time you buy something, ask yourself if six months later you'll look at that purchase and it will make you happy. Or go through your credit card statement line by line and ask the same thing. Remind yourself every time you are about to buy something, what else you could spend that money on, the opportunity cost, and then make the decision that will make you the happiest. This doesn't mean you can't ever buy stuff, but it means you need to be **intentional** about it. Every **$100 in spending per month that you can cut** out will turn into **$150,000 thirty years from**

now (assuming you invest the $100 every month and earn 8% annual return). **That's** opportunity cost.

- Be more explicit with your goals. Instead of saying, "I want to save more", say "I want to save x% of my income so that we can buy a house in three years."

Again, this could go on for a while, but I'll cut it short. A lot of folks want to know how much they should save. 10% of what they make? 15%? For me, that's the wrong way to go about it. You should figure out what makes you happy, what kind of life you want to live, what your goals are, and then act (and spend, and save) accordingly.

I will say that for anyone making a middle class or better income, I think saving 10% is way too low. Most of us managed to live on less than 50% of what we're making now (in college, or when we first moved out on our own), and life was still pretty good. Get off of the hedonic treadmill, avoid lifestyle creep, and make intentional choices and you'll find that you can save much more than you thought possible. While intentional spending in every area is important, housing, transportation and food are the "big rocks" that make the most difference, and we'll talk about those a bit later.

Next we'll talk about some of the specific financial "infrastructure" decisions you might want to make.

1.5: BANK ACCOUNTS

TL;DR: You need a checking and a savings account. You should not be paying any fees for just having those accounts, and they should be earning competitive interest.

"You're better off not giving the small things more time than they deserve." – Marcus Aurelius

Most people need two - and only two - accounts at their bank or credit union. A checking account and a savings account. There are lots of good choices of banks or credit unions depending on where you live and where you work, but here are the non-negotiables:

- Your checking account needs to be **free**. No fees just for having the account open, and no minimum balance. It's okay if it requires a direct deposit, because you should be having your paycheck direct-deposited into the account. Ideally, your checking account would even earn a little interest.

- Your savings account also needs to be free, with no fees and no minimum balance. It should earn interest, and the amount of interest it earns should be competitive with the other choices out there.

If you're not sure if your current accounts meet these criteria, look into it. As of this writing, a good bank to compare to is Ally Bank (**ally.com**). Compare your current accounts to Ally's Checking and Savings accounts (which have no fees and both pay interest), including the interest they are earning. If there is a significant difference, or if there are fees attached to your current accounts, switch. Note that it doesn't have to be Ally, that's just a good comparison as of this writing.

1.6: CREDIT CARDS & LOANS

TL;DR: *Credit cards can be the downfall of your finances or they can be a way to enhance your finances. It all depends on how you use them.*

"What lies in our power to do, lies in our power not to do."
— *Aristotle*

Used poorly, credit cards get a lot of folks in trouble. Used well, credit cards can be a valuable way to not only track and manage your spending, but to actually increase your savings. You know yourself better than anyone, so figure out whether you can be the type of person that uses them well, or not. If not, then it's probably best not to have one (or perhaps to have one for emergencies that you don't carry with you) and only use cash, checks and debit cards. Set up the credit card so that the full balance is paid automatically from your checking account each month, no matter what, and then go on with your life.

If you're disciplined enough to use credit cards well, then take advantage of them. There are many credit cards that actually pay you to use them, through signup bonuses and cash back offers. The reason they do this, of course, is to take advantage of folks who will then spend more and/or not pay off their balances each month and therefore pay interest, so you only want to take advantage of these offers if that won't be you.

There are many websites you can visit to compare current credit card offers (see **fischlearning.com/tldr** for links) but, in general, pick the cards that offer you rewards in the categories that best match your spending, and the ones that offer you cash back as opposed to points to be used toward other purchases. For example, most people spend (or at least they should spend) a significant portion of their income on groceries, so having a credit card that gives you extra cash back at the grocery store you frequent is an obvious choice.

> **Note**: there are some people who use credit cards well for travel hacking where you will want to accumulate points and spend them later on travel - if you spend a lot on traveling, you might go in this direction instead of cash back.

If you're disciplined, there's no reason you can't have multiple cards that offer rewards in different categories and you simply use the appropriate card in the appropriate places. Stagger when you get the cards so you can take advantage of the signup bonuses (typically requires a minimum spend in a certain amount of time), and keep an eye on your credit score so you don't open up too many, too fast. But as long as you set them all to pay off automatically each month, having multiple credit cards can actually increase your credit score because part of the calculation for your score is the amount of available credit you are using. See **bit.ly/tldrcc1** and **bit.ly/tldrcc2** for more.)

Credit cards are also helpful as a way to keep track of your spending, so you can identify areas where you are perhaps spending more than you thought. It's easy when spending cash, or even using a debit card, to not notice how much you are spending on Starbucks (as just one example, not trying to pick on Starbucks). But if you use a credit card, and then take a moment to examine your statement each month, you'll get a better idea of what you are actually spending money on. You can even use free tools like **Personal Capital (personalcapital.com)** that you can set up to automatically bring in your accounts and it will keep track for you. Review the categories in light of opportunity costs and your definition of the good life, and go from there.

A brief note about loans: try to avoid them. In a tl;dr book, we can't go into the complexities of loans but, much like with the discussion of spending and the use of credit cards above, if you live within (hopefully well within) your means, you shouldn't have to resort to getting a loan very often (if at all).

Obviously, if you choose to buy a house, the vast majority of folks will have to take out a mortgage. If owning a home is part of the life you want to live, then that would be a "good" loan to get. (In general, for mortgages you want to get the lowest fixed rate mortgage you can.) Lots of folks think a car loan is a necessity but, as discussed in the next section, it might not be. If you have to have a car and can't afford to pay cash for it, then buy a reliable, used car, pay as much cash as you can, then get a loan for the rest that you pay off as quickly as you can. Once you have that first car you should be able to avoid loans for any future car purchases.

1.7: HOUSING, TRANSPORTATION & FOOD

TL;DR: Conventional wisdom on where to live, what to live in, what to drive, and where and what to eat is often wrong, or at least not thoughtful and intentional enough. Take some time to match your choices with your definition of the good life.

"It is not that we have so little time but that we lose so much." — Seneca

Conventional wisdom...

- "Buy a house as soon as you can."

- "Buy as big of a house as you can afford."

- "Move-up to a bigger, nicer house as soon as you can afford to."

- "Buy a nice car that holds its value and makes your commute as enjoyable as possible."

- "We 'deserve' to eat out."

All of these statements might fall under "conventional wisdom", and all of them are wrong for a significant number of people. To be clear, **they may not be wrong for you**, but housing, transportation and food are three of the biggest and most consequential financial decisions you make in your life and they have an outsized effect on the quality of your life, so it's important to get these right.

Like all other financial decisions, you should make these in the context of the good life you want to live and what truly makes you happy. The so-called "American Dream" tends to include owning your own (large) house with a nice lawn, and several late-model cars in the driveway, that you use to take you to restaurants to eat out frequently. If that's truly what you want, there's nothing wrong with that. But, for many (perhaps most) folks, those decisions are often made on autopilot and don't actually align with their version of the good life.

Some things for you to consider and research more:

- For a lot of folks, home ownership is actually less convenient, more restrictive, and more expensive than renting. The conventional wisdom that renting is throwing your money away while owning is investing can be correct, but often is not. And when you add in the time and hassle requirements of owning a home, renting is often the better choice.

- If you do decide to buy a house, try to "right-size" it the first time. Every time you "move-up" to a new house, the transaction costs can be expensive, not to mention the increased time and spending associated with moving. That doesn't necessarily mean "buy the biggest house you can afford", it means trying to figure out what size house you will need for the size of family you'll have, and then waiting to purchase until you can afford that house.

- Research consistently shows that commute times are negatively correlated with happiness and are one of the biggest impediments to happiness. The longer the commute, the less happier people are. This is a huge issue that most folks don't think about when choosing where to live. Yes, folks will look for a house within a reasonable commute of their work, but give some more thought to what "reasonable" really is. And if you can, live close enough to work that you don't need to use a car at all (walk, bike, or use public transportation - it will not only save you a ton of money, it will improve your health).

• In addition to robbing you of happiness, commutes are expensive. Don't assume you have to own a car, or multiple cars. Think carefully about where you are going to live in relation to where you work. This one decision - finding a place to live near where you work - can be **the** deciding factor in your financial success. Most folks have no idea how much they truly spend on their cars over their lifetime. Eliminating or reducing this increases happiness and financial well-being.

• If you do end up buying a car (or two or three), think carefully about what you need. In the United States, SUV's and Heavy-Duty Pickup trucks are really, really popular. But most people don't need those capabilities for their daily commute, only for occasional use. (Pro-tip: two parents and up to three kids can truly fit in a typical sedan - depending on their respective ages and number of car seats you need at any one time.) Consider purchasing a more economical vehicle (both in terms of purchase price and operating costs) and, on the occasions when you need the SUV or pickup, rent one. You'll come out way ahead in the end. (And, as I write this, buying an electric vehicle is probably the best choice not only for the environment, but for your finances, as they have a much lower total cost of ownership.)

• One place where conventional wisdom is usually correct is buying used vehicles versus new. The quality of cars has increased dramatically in the last 20 years, so buying a three, five, or eight-year-old car is not that risky these days, and can save you a lot of money. This is especially helpful if you are also making choices that minimize how much you have to use the car, as that will increase its effective lifespan. Buy used, buy economical, drive less, and keep for as long as it runs will have huge positive effects on your finances and your happiness.

● Think carefully about food and the value (to you) of eating out. While there's nothing wrong with eating out occasionally, it is incredibly more expensive than eating at home. Many Americans have gotten in the habit of eating as many meals (or more) out as they do at home, and that's had disastrous effects on their finances. Evaluate whether what you really value is eating the food at the restaurant, or eating good food with family and good friends. If it's the latter, you can almost certainly spend much less money, eat just as well, and actually have a better time at home.

Don't assume you have to buy a house or a car, and don't assume you have to go out to eat to have a good time. If you do, don't assume you have to spend as much on those things as others think you do. And pay very careful attention to the location of where you live compared to where you work. It's important enough that you should consider changing either where you live or where you work to minimize your commute and your expenses. It's truly that important.

1.8: INSURANCE

TL;DR: The purpose of insurance is to protect you against large expenses, not to "pay for stuff". Buy the least expensive insurance that adequately accomplishes that task.

"We should always be asking ourselves: 'Is this something that is, or is not, in my control?'" —Epictetus

Many folks in my generation grew up with the idea that insurance was supposed to pay for things. Particularly when it came to medical insurance, the feeling was that insurance should pay for everything - or almost everything - and we (individuals) should pay very little. Setting aside any political viewpoints, under our current system this just isn't possible.

Insurance companies have to make enough money to cover expenses (which includes any claims you make plus the overhead of administering the program) and, if they are for-profit, have to make a profit above and beyond that. The only way to do that is to make sure the combination of the premiums you pay plus any out-of-pocket expenses you pay adds up to at least what their expenses are plus whatever profit they make. Your employer likely covers at least some of your premium (for health, dental and perhaps vision insurance), but you have to pay the rest. Most employers offer at least some choice of plans, with the differences between the plans mostly a tradeoff between a higher premium with lower out-of-pocket expenses or a lower premium with higher out-of-pocket expenses.

Every individual's situation is unique, of course, but generally you want to purchase the least expensive insurance that protects you from **catastrophic** expenses. That's the original idea behind insurance, that a group of people pool their money so that when something unfortunate happens to one person, their life isn't ruined. For that to happen, however, there have to be other people who end up paying **more** for insurance than for the benefit they actually receive. Instead of looking at insurance as "paying for things", try to reframe your thinking to insurance as "protecting against catastrophe." You are going to need to pay for the things you use, insurance is there for the hopefully uncommon occurrence of massive expenses (your house burns down, you have a major medical condition, etc.)

If you make your insurance choices with that mindset, you will most likely choose to increase your deductibles (whether that be for car, house or medical) in exchange for lower premiums. That still provides you the security that if something tragic and expensive occurs, it won't bankrupt you, while paying for the services you use. It will also likely lower your premiums for insurance, which provides you extra cash along the way, but it's really important to set aside that cash to cover the increased out-of-pocket expenses you may have. (If you have a high-deductible health plan, for example, I would highly recommend you put any premium savings into an HSA, which is discussed later).

So, consider raising the deductible on your auto and home/renters insurance. Consider a high-deductible health care plan and put the premium savings into an HSA. And, perhaps most importantly, try to live your life in a way that decreases the risks that you have a large claim. Drive responsibly, wear your seatbelt, eat right and exercise. All of those things will not only make your life better, but make it much more likely you won't have to pay those out-of-pocket expenses to reach your deductible.

1.9: TAXES

TL;DR: For most people, taxes aren't very complicated. There are some simple things you can do to minimize the taxes you pay but, for the most part, don't spend a lot of time thinking (or worrying) about taxes.

"In America, there are two tax systems; one for the informed and one for the uninformed. Both systems are legal." —Judge Learned Hand

For the majority of folks, taxes should be pretty simple these days. You're most likely going to take the standard deduction at the federal level, so the only things to think about are ways to minimize your taxable income and occasionally to take advantage of special tax incentives (e.g., **Savers Credit**, or the tax credit for purchasing an electric vehicle). Even if you do have enough deductions to itemize, it's probably worth more of your time to think about minimizing your taxable income.

Obviously in a book like this I'm not going to cover all the ins-and-outs of the tax code, but let's just hit the highlights of what you want to consider. For most people, the main ways to minimize your taxable income is to contribute to a 401k/403b/457/IRA/FSA/Dependent Care Spending Account/etc., make sure any health insurance premiums you pay through your employer come out pre-tax and, if you have a high-deductible health care plan, contribute as much as you can to your HSA.

We'll talk more about tax-advantaged savings plans below but, for the purposes of this section, here's what you need to know. Any money you contribute to a traditional 401k/403b/457/IRA plan comes out pre-tax, which means you won't have to pay any federal or state income taxes on that money in the year that you earn it. (Keep in mind you will end up eventually paying taxes when you withdraw it, hopefully many years in the future during retirement). So, for example, if you are in the 22% federal tax bracket, for every $100 you contribute to your traditional 401k/403b/457/IRA plan, your net paycheck with only go down by $78 (because you won't be withholding/paying $22 in taxes to the U.S. government).

But it gets even better, because your state also gives you a tax break. So depending on what tax bracket you are in for your state, your net paycheck will go down even less. For example, Colorado has a flat rate of 4.40%, so if you're in the 22% federal tax bracket, for every $100 you contribute your net paycheck will only go down by $73.60. Note that if you are part of a pension plan, 401k/403b/457 contributions typically do not reduce your pension contribution, but your pension contribution itself comes out before federal and state taxes are assessed.

Many employers also offer a Roth version of 401k/403b/457 plans, plus you can invest in a Roth IRA outside of your employer. These dollars are post-tax, meaning you don't get a tax break now, but any earnings and future withdrawals are tax free. Depending on your income, current tax bracket, expected pension or social security benefits, and future tax rates, it may make sense to split your money between the traditional (pre-tax) and Roth (post-tax) plans.

In addition to any contributions you make to a retirement plan, most employers allow you to choose to pay insurance premiums with pre-tax money (referred to as **Section 125 plans**). Very few people should choose not to take advantage of this, so check your pay stub or with your Human Resources department to make sure you are. You can also have money for child care expenses and flexible spending accounts pulled out pre-tax, and you should definitely take advantage of those when you can. (One notable exception: for some pension plans you may want to stop paying premiums and having other deductions come out pre-tax during your last years of service in order to maximize your pension benefit.)

Finally, if you have a high-deductible health care plan, you will want to take advantage of **Health Savings Accounts** (HSAs). These are known as "triple-tax-advantaged" plans, because not only are your contributions pre-tax, but your savings can be invested and grown tax free, and then your withdrawals are also tax free if used for medical expenses. In other words, you **never** pay tax on this money. Often employers will contribute a small amount to your HSA, but you can also choose to contribute out of your paycheck. The more you contribute (within the federal limit), the lower your taxes will be.

> **Note**: Remember, **HSA** accounts values carry over at the end of the calendar year, but money left in **FSA** accounts is surrendered. Make sure you are clear which you are funding.

Not only will you pay less in taxes if you lower your taxable income, but lowering your taxable income often allows you to qualify for more tax credits, which lowers the taxes you have to pay even more. Many tax credits (incentives) have an income limit where they get phased out and, for some of them, all of the above pre-tax contributions are taken into account when calculating that limit. So by lowering your taxable income, you just might qualify for more tax credits (the Savers Credit is a good one to look at, particularly at the beginning of your career when you are not making as much).

> **Quick reminder**: The information in this book is not a substitute for contacting a tax professional. Please contact a tax professional to clarify and confirm your plan before acting!

1.10: INVESTING: ASSET ALLOCATION

TL;DR: Next to the amount you save, the most important part of investing isn't choosing the individual investments, it's choosing your asset allocation. How you divide up your investments among different types of assets (stocks, bonds, etc.) is the main determiner of your investment returns.

"The fox knows many things, but the hedgehog knows one big thing." — *Archilochus*

Choosing investments freaks people out. There is so much information out there that it can be overwhelming and, because they fear making a "mistake", many people end up making poor investment decisions by not making any investment decisions. The good news is that it really isn't that difficult, you just have to make a few pretty simple decisions and perhaps make some small adjustments over time. That's it.

One can devise a really complicated investment strategy, using lots of different asset classes and lots of exotic products, but those complicated investment strategies rarely (if ever) pay off. In fact, the vast majority of investors will earn better investment returns by sticking with a simple, low-cost asset allocation consisting of stocks and bonds. If you really get into investing and want to tweak your portfolio and invest in additional asset classes, you can maybe squeeze a little bit more return over time, but you're also just as likely (probably more likely) to underperform.

So here's what 95% of investors should do. Save as much as you can and invest it in perhaps three different "buckets": a **short-term bucket**, a **medium-term bucket**, and a **long-term bucket**. As always, individual circumstances vary but, in general, any money that you think you might want to spend in the next five or so years you should consider a short-term investment (really more savings than investment), in five to fifteen years a medium-term investment, and all other investment money (typically retirement) consider a long-term investment. Your asset allocation for each bucket will be different, with the short-term bucket invested much more conservatively and your long-term bucket invested much more aggressively, and the medium-term in between. (Don't let the choice of the term "aggressive" frighten you, it simply means that since you are investing for the long-term, you can tolerate any short-term drop in the markets.)

How you divide up your investments in each bucket depends on your tolerance for risk. This is really mostly looking at the risk of *your own behavior* undermining your investment returns. If you invest more "aggressively" and the markets go down, will you freak out and sell (and therefore be "buying high and selling low")? If so, then you might set your asset allocation more conservatively. If you understand how markets work long term, and therefore control your own behavior, you can invest more "aggressively" and therefore earn a higher return over time. (Again, investing "aggressively" doesn't mean you're being unduly risky, it just means you are investing in assets that will have a better return over the long-term, with the chance that they will be more volatile in the short-term.)

So, what does this look like? Again, individual circumstances matter, but here's a good place to start. Your short-term bucket is money you plan on spending in the next five years or so. A common example of this is saving for a down-payment on a house (or perhaps to buy a car). Because stocks can go down and stay down for a while, you generally don't want very much of this money invested in stocks. So your short-term bucket should be invested primarily in bonds, perhaps certificates of deposits, and your savings account. You may want to have a relatively small percentage invested in stocks as well (see the next section for more on this).

For your medium-term bucket, money you'll spend in the next five to fifteen years (typical example: saving for a child's college education), you want to have a mix of stocks and bonds that perhaps begins to shift more to bonds the closer you get to the anticipated spend date (e.g., college admission).

For the long-term bucket, money you don't anticipate needing for a long time (for example, for retirement), you want to invest it mostly in stocks (again, depending on your risk tolerance and your own likely behavior in a market downturn). Since this money is going to be used a long time in the future, you can ride out the ups-and-downs of the stock market and earn a higher rate of return by investing more in stocks and less in bonds. As you approach your spending date (e.g., retirement), you might start to shift your allocation to look more like your medium or short-term buckets.

It really is that simple. You don't have to be a fox and know lots of things about investing, just a hedgehog who understands their buckets and picks the right asset allocation. In the next section I'll talk more about how much of each bucket to put into stocks and how much into bonds, and what specific investments you should choose, but the takeaway from this section is pretty simple: save as much as you can and invest it based on the time-horizon of when you are going to need to spend the money.

> **Quick reminder**: The information in this book is not a substitute for researching and using your own critical thinking. Please contact a fiduciary to help clarify and confirm your plan before acting! I am NOT a certified financial planners, but aim to help you start your education!

1.11: INVESTING: SPECIFIC INVESTMENTS

TL;DR: *Decide on your asset allocation for each bucket, and invest in low-cost index funds. Keep it simple.*

"Put 10% of the cash in short-term government bonds and 90% in a very low-cost S&P 500 index fund. (I suggest Vanguard's.) I believe the trust's long-term results from this policy will be superior to those attained by most investors —whether pension funds, institutions or individuals—who employ high-fee managers." — Warren Buffett

As discussed in the previous section, divide your investments into a short-term bucket (want to spend it in five years or less), a medium-term bucket (five to fifteen years), and a long-term bucket. For your short-term bucket, you want a more "conservative" asset allocation (bonds, certificates of deposit, and savings), for the medium-term bucket more of a balanced asset allocation (stocks and bonds), and for your long-term bucket a more "aggressive" allocation (more stocks). The specific allocation you decide on will depend on your risk tolerance, but the following is some general advice.

In general, humans are loss-averse, they worry more about losing (in this case, losing money) than winning, and will do whatever it takes to avoid that. As a result, most investors have an asset allocation that is too conservative. If you are a long-term investor (which you should be) and will not panic and sell before you need the money, then you should be invested mostly in stocks in your long-term bucket. In your short-term bucket, invest mostly in bonds (although as you get closer to the spend-date, consider certificates of deposit or your savings account for any new money).

For both stocks and bonds, you should invest in low-cost, diversified index funds. While there are several good choices, it's best to keep it simple. For investments you have complete control over (typically your non-tax advantaged accounts, your Roth IRA, and your traditional IRA if you have one), go with **Vanguard**. For your tax-advantaged accounts through your employer (401k/403b/457 and possibly an HSA), you will be limited by the choices the plan offers you. If Vanguard is a choice, go with them. If not, most plans have an **index fund choice from somebody**, so choose that (or the choice that's closest to that with the **lowest expense ratio**). While you can't control what the market does, you can control your expenses, which is why choosing low-cost index funds (which have lower expenses) will pay off in the long run.

> **Note**: There are good choices other than Vanguard, but they are consistently one of the best (or the best). They are the only mutual fund company owned by their customers (you), and this helps them keep fees low and always operate in your best interest.

So, what should your asset allocation look like? Again, it's going to vary, but here are some good baselines. For each of these, I take a "white-label" approach, by choosing the type of asset as opposed to a particular fund. This is helpful because within your employer-based plan you will likely have the choices of funds determined for you, so you can pick the fund(s) that most closely match the "white-label". For each "white-label" I also give the specific symbol for the Vanguard fund associated with it as a **reference** (you can use funds or ETFs, whichever is easier for you). I break down each bucket into different portfolio choices: a one fund, a target-date fund, a three fund, and a five fund choice. Most people will be best served with fewer funds, but if you just have to have a little more, the five fund choice is there for you.

Note: As you get closer to the time when you are needing to spend the money in the long-term bucket, you may want to start adjusting it closer to the short-term bucket asset allocation. That will really depend on your financial situation at that time.

Short-Term Bucket

- **One Fund**: Total Bond Market Index Fund (VBTLX)

- **Target Date Fund**: Choose the closest date to when you want to spend the money (e.g., if you anticipate spending the money in 2026, choose a Target Date 2025 fund (VTTVX).

- **Three Fund**: Total Bond Market Index Fund (VBTLX), Certificates of Deposit (timed to redeem when you need to spend the money), Savings Account

- **Five Fund**: Total Bond Market Index Fund (VBTLX), Certificates of Deposit (timed to redeem when you need to spend the money), Savings Account, High-Yield Bond Fund (VWEAX), Total Stock Market Index Fund (VTSAX)

Medium-Term Bucket

- **One Fund**: Balanced Fund (VSMGX)

- **Target Date Fund**: Choose the closest date to when you want to spend the money (e.g., if you anticipate spending the money in 2026, choose a Target Date 2025 fund (VTTVX).

- **Three Fund**: Total Stock Market Index Fund (VTSAX), Total International Stock Index Fund (VTIAX), Total Bond Market Index Fund (VBTLX)

- **Five Fund**: Total Stock Market Index Fund (VTSAX), Total International Stock Index Fund (VTIAX), Real Estate Index

Fund (VGSLX), Total Bond Market Index Fund (VBTLX), High-Yield Bond Fund (VWEAX)

Long-Term Bucket

- **One Fund**: Total Stock Market Index Fund (VTSAX)

- **Target Date Fund**: Take the year you anticipate needing to spend the money (e.g., when you are going to retire), and add five or ten years. So, for example, if you anticipate retiring in 2050, perhaps pick a Target 2055 or 2060 account (TL;DR for the explanation of why you should add five or ten years).

- **Three Fund**: Total Stock Market Index Fund (VTSAX), Total International Stock Index Fund (VTIAX), Real Estate Index Fund (VGSLX)

- **Five Fund**: Total Stock Market Index Fund (VTSAX), Total International Stock Index Fund (VTIAX), Emerging Markets Stock Index Fund (VEMAX), Small Cap Value Index Fund (VSIAX), Real Estate Index Fund (VGSLX)

For all of the multiple fund choices, you would periodically **rebalance** between the different funds to stay within your risk tolerance (and to force you to "sell high, buy low" because you'd be selling the funds that went up the most and buying the ones that went up the least). Again, don't stress out about making these investment choices. If you focus on your savings rate, and start investing early, time is your ally. While it's unclear if he ever actually said it, Albert Einstein is purported to have said, "Compound interest is the most powerful force in the universe." Whether he said it or not, it is one of the most powerful forces in your financial universe. If you **save early**, **invest in index funds**, and **continue saving and investing throughout your life**, compound interest will take care of the rest.

1.12: INVESTING: WHAT TYPE OF ACCOUNTS TO INVEST IN

TL;DR: This can be really complicated, so tough to tl;dr it. In general, short and medium-term bucket investments will be in taxable accounts, and long-term bucket investments will be in tax-advantaged accounts.

"A tax loophole is something that benefits the other guy. If it benefits you, it's tax reform." — Senator Russell Long

This is a very difficult section to tl;dr, as your decisions will vary tremendously based on your goals, your current circumstances, and what options you have available to you based on your employment. Consider the following a general introduction and then see **fischlearning.com/tldr** for resources to dive deeper.

Once you decide on your asset allocation and your various buckets, you then have to decide in what types of accounts to invest in. Mainly, this is a decision about whether to invest intaxable accounts or tax-advantaged accounts (401k, Roth IRA, etc.), and then within those tax-advantaged accounts which type(s) to invest in.

In general, your short and medium-term bucket investments will be in taxable accounts (notable exception: college savings, more on that later). Your long-term bucket investments will be invested in a combination of taxable and tax-advantaged accounts, and most likely multiple types of tax-advantaged accounts. Your exact choices here will vary a lot depending on your individual circumstances and goals.

For example, if you want to retire early you will have a different mix of accounts than if you plan on retiring at a "regular" age. Or if your employer matches some of your contributions to your 401k that might change your mix a bit. Similarly, if you get a pension from your employment, that can have dramatic effects on what you choose to do (and your asset allocation). But, in general, for **many** (but **not all**) folks, the priority order will be:

- 401k (403b/457) up to company match

- HSA (if you are enrolled in a High-Deductible Health Care Plan)

- Traditional and/or Roth IRA

- Traditional and/or Roth 401k (403b/457) up to the maximum you're allowed (If you are a public employee with access to a 401k/403b **and** a 457, you can double the amount you invest as each has its own limit).

- Taxable brokerage account

Money that you invest in your Traditional 401k (403b/457) comes out pre-tax and then grows tax free and is then taxed when you withdraw it during retirement. By coming out pre-tax, it allows you to invest "more" because you are able to invest what you would've paid in federal and state (and maybe local) taxes. And, if your employer matches any of your contribution, it's equivalent to getting a tax-free raise. In addition, because your contributions lower your adjusted gross income and taxable income, it can help qualify you for other tax breaks that you might not receive if you didn't invest in the 401k (e.g., Savers Credit, lower capital gains taxes, etc.).

Once you've invested at least enough to obtain your employer's match and if you have a High-Deductible Health Plan, then invest the next amount in your HSA. Recall that you can withdraw funds from your HSA to pay health expenses but, if you can manage to not use the money to pay current health care expenses, it's a great long-term investment vehicle because the money is never taxed (comes out pre-tax, grows tax-free, and withdrawal is tax free if used for health expenses down the road). If used this way, it's like a "stealth" retirement account - and the only one that is never taxed.

After you've invested in your HSA, then often the next thing to do is to max out your Traditional or Roth IRA. This is because if you choose some place like Vanguard and choose low-cost, diversified index funds, the fees you pay will likely be less than through your employer 401k/403b/457. Note that there are income limits for being able to contribute to a Traditional or Roth IRA, so you may not be able to take advantage of this.

After that, then make sure you have maxed out your 401k (403b/457) contribution. If you are a public employee and have access to both a 401k/403b and a 457, realize that the maximum investment limits for those are separate, so you can invest in both (effectively doubling the amount you can invest pre-tax). Also, assuming the investment choices and fees are equal, public employees should usually fund a 457 before a 401k/403b, because it's easier to withdraw your money earlier if you need to.

Once you've maxed out your pre-tax accounts, then any remaining money you have to invest can be invested in a taxable brokerage account (again, in diversified, low-cost index funds at a vendor like Vanguard).

Again, a reminder that this is general advice and the priority order can be different depending on your individual circumstances, investment choices, and retirement age (see **fischlearning.com/tldr** for additional resources).

1.13: INVESTING FOR COLLEGE

TL;DR: For most people, investing in a 529 College Savings Plan, typically (but not always) in the state you live, is the best option for saving for college.

"An investment in knowledge always pays the best interest." — Benjamin Franklin

If you decide to have children you will likely want to start saving and investing some money to help pay for their possible college education. For most people a **529 plan** is the best way to save for a college education for your child(ren). Earnings in a 529 plan grow tax-free and withdrawals are not taxed as long as they are used for college expenses. Some states also offer some kind of state tax incentive on contributions (e.g., in Colorado any contributions to 529 plans come out **pre-Colorado-state-tax**, meaning you automatically earn a **4.40% return on investment just for contributing**). Colorado's First Step Program will also give you $100 when you open your account and match up to $1,000 in contributions during your child's first five years (see **bit.ly/cofirststep** for more info).

You can invest in any 529 plan, not just the one offered by your state. If your state doesn't offer any special incentives, then shop around the other states and pick the plan that has the best choice of index funds with low expense ratios (**savingforcollege.com** is a great resource to help you learn more).

When it comes time to pay for college, you can withdraw money from the 529 plan without any tax consequences. Keep in mind that you do want to optimize for any other tuition assistance that might be available for you. For example, right now you can get up to a $2,500 tax credit through the **American Opportunity Tax Credit** (phased out for higher incomes), but you can only get that credit if you don't use 529 money for $4,000 worth of expenses (the first $2,000 is dollar-for-dollar tax credit, the next $2,000 is $0.25 for each dollar of expenses tax credit). So, for many folks, paying $4,000 a year with regular savings (not from the 529 account) and then using 529 money for anything above that makes the most sense.

1.14: EMPLOYMENT

TL;DR: Spend the time to learn about the benefits your employer offers and then make the optimal choices. Many people don't think deeply enough about their choices or take full advantage of their benefits.

"Workin' 9 to 5, what a way to make a livin'
Barely gettin' by, it's all takin' and no givin'
They just use your mind and they never give you credit
It's enough to drive you crazy if you let it"
— Dolly Parton

There is lots of advice out there about what kind of job you should get. Some folks advocate pursuing your passion, others doing what you are good at, and still others to do whatever will make you the most money. No matter which approach you take, once you have a job then you want to maximize the financial benefit you receive from that job.

Obviously, pay is important. The higher your salary or hourly wage, the more control over your financial situation you'll have. In many jobs, you can do what's expected of you and be just fine. But in some jobs, if you go above and beyond, you can increase your pay. Often your best option is to invest in yourself, learning additional skills and abilities that will allow you to perform your job better or even advance to another job within (or outside of) the company. If you continue to grow, your pay will typically grow with you.

While pay is the obvious part of work that most people focus on, many folks only think about benefits when they first get a job (or when they complain about them). And, often, those benefit choices are made quickly and without a lot of thought because you're excited about the new job and just want to get started. It is really worth your time to set aside an hour or so and dive a bit deeper into your benefits.

As mentioned previously, choosing your insurance options should require a bit more thinking than simply choosing the lowest premium or the lowest out-of-pocket cost. Often a plan with higher deductibles (like a high-deductible health plan) is the unintuitively better choice. You also want to take advantage of any other benefits your employer offers, such as taking out your insurance premiums pre-tax, or taking advantage of flexible spending accounts (health care, limited purpose health care, dependent care spending, etc.), known collectively as Section 125 plans.

You definitely want to take advantage of any employer matching for a 401k/403b/457 or company stock purchase program. (And you want to review the previous investment sections when looking at the investment choices in your 401k/403b/457 plan.) Some employers even offer help with covering your commuting costs, such as discounts on public transportation.

Just a reminder to also think carefully about the location of your work compared to where you live. As mentioned previously, your daily commute has an outsized impact on both your happiness and your finances. The more you can minimize your commute, and perhaps eliminate the need to drive to work every day, the better off financially you will be.

Finally, a quick note about **working while in high school and college**. Many folks have to work in high school or college to help their family pay the bills. But, for students who are lucky and privileged enough to not have to use that money to pay the bills, they should seriously consider **opening and contributing to a Roth IRA** during these years.

Because most students in high school or college will not make enough to owe any federal taxes, taking this opportunity to invest in a Roth IRA means that money will **never be taxed** (they might have to pay a small amount in state taxes depending on their state). And, because they're young, that leaves plenty of time for compound interest to do its magic. They should also consider talking with their parents about possibly matching some or all of their contribution to the Roth IRA (kind of like an "employer match", only from their parents), so that they still have some "spending" money. They should try to contribute as much as possible to their Roth IRA (up to the limit, which is currently their total earned income for the year up to $6,000 maximum, including any "match" from their parents).

I'd also highly recommend that if you have your own high school or college-aged children, have them **read Part 1 of this book**, and then discuss it with them. Or, alternatively, you could buy them the standalone **TL;DR: Financial Literacy for Young (and Not-So-Young) Adults (bit.ly/fischtldr)**, which is essentially Part 1 of this book without the PERA references. Imagine the possibilities if they start their adult lives being financially literate. (See **bit.ly/teensandroth** for more on this.)

1.15: RETIREMENT

TL;DR: The key to a comfortable retirement is to save and invest early and let compound interest go to work.

"For it is in your power to retire into yourself whenever you choose."— Marcus Aurelius

I'm only going to briefly mention retirement in this section, as we will delve more deeply into it in the following three sections.

Having said that, the best way to assure that you will be able to retire comfortably when you want to is to start planning (and saving, and investing) **early**. If you follow the advice in this book, as well as learn a little bit more after this, you are well on your way. When you can retire depends on a variety of factors, but the most important one is how much you save (which, as discussed previously, is based on how much you spend). The more you save and invest - particularly if you start early and let compound interest do its magic - the earlier you will be able to retire. Note that you may not want to "retire early", but reaching a "**work optional**" stage of life earlier rather than later is appealing for most folks. (Again, it more likely allows you to live the life you want to live.) There is a whole community online known as the FIRE community (Financial Independence Retire Early) that you can explore if you want to learn more about reaching that work optional (financially independent) stage earlier.

PART 2: YOUR PERA BENEFITS

Note that this will not cover every intricacy and detail of your PERA benefits, but will cover the most important aspects. Please always check out **copera.org** or contact PERA directly with any questions (they are very, very helpful). As of this writing, you can find detailed booklets on many of the following topics at **copera.org/member-and-retiree-forms.** Also keep in mind that PERA benefits can change over time.

2.1: WHAT IS PERA AND WHAT DOES IT PROVIDE FOR ME?

TL;DR: While an incredibly important part of your PERA Membership, your defined benefit (your pension) is only one part of the many valuable benefits PERA Membership provides.

Colorado Public Employees' Retirement Association **(PERA)** was created in 1931 by the state of Colorado to provide retirement benefits to public employees in the state of Colorado. It predates Social Security and is actually a **substitute** for Social Security for public employees in Colorado (most PERA members do not pay into Social Security while working for a PERA employer).

PERA members include employees of the state of Colorado, all public school districts, judges in the Colorado judicial system, and many municipalities, special districts, public health departments, and other local government entities. While the rules and benefits are very similar across these different divisions of PERA, there are differences that can be important. For the rest of Part 2, we will focus **solely on public school district members** (the "school division" of PERA). If you are a PERA member in another division, the majority of what follows applies to you as well, but you should check to see what differences there may be. (Note that Denver Public Schools employees have slightly different rules than the rest of the school division, but we will not cover those differences here.)

PERA is a "Hybrid Defined Benefit Plan" but, for public school employees, it functions solely as a Defined Benefit (DB) Plan. A **Defined Benefit Plan** means that you receive a lifetime retirement benefit determined by a formula that is based on the number of **years of employment**, your **highest average salary (HAS)**, and the **age at which you retire**. This is in contrast to a **Defined Contribution Plan (DC)** like a 401k (or similar plan like a 403b/457), where your retirement benefit is dependent on how much you save and invest and how those investments grow, and where your retirement benefit can be exhausted when your personal account is depleted.

Your lifetime benefit is paid for by contributions both you and your employer make to PERA, as well as the investment gains those contributions earn over time. There are over 600,000 members of PERA and it currently has over $50 billion in assets invested on behalf of its members. Because it invests on behalf of all those members, PERA has the advantage of being a truly long-term investor and can ride out the volatility that occurs in the market. Because PERA is so large, it is able to both invest at low cost and to invest in areas that are not available to you as an individual investor. Because they are a large, institutional investor, they are able to negotiate investment fees that are lower than what you can typically achieve on your own. They can also invest in areas such as real estate and private equity that are not available to you as an individual investor. Both of these help PERA achieve higher returns (at the same level of risk) than most individual investors. As an individual investing in a 401k, you have to account for different risks that are very sensitive to your current age, the rest of your financial situation, and the state of the market. PERA, on the other hand, can invest on behalf of all of its members and its size allows for it to better weather the inevitable ups and downs of the markets.

Public school employees currently contribute 10.5% of their salary (more on what constitutes PERA-includable salary below). There is also an **automatic adjustment provision** that can increase or decrease your contribution based on the current funded status of PERA (typically in 0.5% increments). The automatic adjustment provision will increase the employee contribution to 11% on July 1, 2022.

Your employer (your school district) currently contributes 20.9% of your salary to PERA (this will increase to 21.4% on July 1, 2022). The reason this is so much higher than your contribution is complicated, but for the most part it is to make up for past mistakes in overpromising benefits and underfunding the plan. This is referred to as the "unfunded liability" and the "extra" that the employers are contributing is designed to pay off that unfunded liability within the next 28 years or so. Once that unfunded liability is (hopefully) paid off in the late 2040's, then both employee and employer contributions will likely drop, although that is not guaranteed. (Note that the total employee plus employer contribution is essentially all coming from the employer, so the distinction between the two is only important because the employee contribution counts as more of a liability for the plan because the employee can take that money with them if they leave.)

In addition to the Defined Benefit you receive upon retiring, PERA also offers several additional important benefits, including a **cost of living adjustment** when retired, **Disability and Survivor benefits**, an **optional voluntary retirement savings plan** (tax advantaged 401k and/or 457), an **optional voluntary life insurance plan**, and an **optional health insurance program** when retired (which is partially subsidized). While most members (rightfully) focus on the Defined Benefit piece of PERA, these other benefits are also really important and we will take a look at all of them.

> **Quick reminder**: The information in this book is not a substitute for contacting the system. Please contact PERA to clarify and confirm your plan before acting!

2.2: PERA'S DEFINED BENEFIT PLAN

TL;DR: While most people know they get a pension from PERA, being more knowledgeable about how that pension is calculated can help you maximize your benefit amount.

While most PERA members know they have a "good" pension plan, they may not be aware of how good it is (and also how it affects the rest of your financial planning decisions). The following will give the basics of how your benefit is determined and later we'll talk about some ways to optimize those benefits.

Your retirement benefit is determined based on a formula that combines the **number of years of service** you have with a PERA employer, your **highest average salary** (HAS), the **age at which you retire**, and **when you first started service with a PERA employer**. That last one is critical, because the benefits that employees receive from PERA have changed over time, as the state legislature makes changes to the plan. Most of those changes only apply to new hires, meaning existing PERA employees are "grandfathered" under the old provisions that were in place at the time they were hired.

The date you were **hired** (your membership date) and the date you **vest** in PERA (when you earn **five years** of service credit) impact both your contributions and your benefits. There are (currently) four areas this affects.

Highest Average Salary (HAS) Tables

Based on the date you were hired and the date you vested, different rules apply as to what age you can retire with full retirement benefits, reduced retirement benefits, or no benefits at all (until you age into the reduced or full categories). While links can change, as of this writing you can find the current HAS tables at **copera.org/highest-average-salary-tables**. While the chart below shows the current breakdown, I recommend you go to that link now to determine which HAS table applies to you and then take a look at the table that applies to you to get a better understanding.

HIGHEST AVERAGE SALARY PERCENTAGES TABLES

Please refer to the chart below to determine which table applies to you. *Note:* The shaded areas on the tables indicate reduced retirement percentages. The percentages in the shaded areas on the PERA 2, PERA 4, PERA 6, PERA 7, PERA 8, PERA 9, DPS 3, DPS 4, Safety Officers 2, and Safety Officers 3 tables ensure that, as of your effective date of retirement, your reduced retirement benefit is the actuarial equivalent of your full service retirement benefit. These percentages are subject to change based on actuarial experience.

Benefit Structure	Membership Date	Five Years of Service Credit as of January 1, 2011	Retirement Eligibility	Table
PERA	On or before June 30, 2005	Yes	Eligible January 1, 2011	PERA 1
PERA	On or before June 30, 2005	Yes	Not eligible January 1, 2011	PERA 2
PERA	Between July 1, 2005, and December 31, 2006	Yes	Eligible January 1, 2011	PERA 3
PERA	Between July 1, 2005, and December 31, 2006	Yes	Not eligible January 1, 2011	PERA 4
PERA	Between January 1, 2007, and December 31, 2010	N/A	Eligible January 1, 2011	PERA 5
PERA	Between January 1, 2007, and December 31, 2010	N/A	Not eligible January 1, 2011	PERA 6
PERA	On or before December 31, 2006	No	N/A	PERA 6
PERA	Between January 1, 2011, and December 31, 2016	N/A	N/A	PERA 7
PERA	Between January 1, 2017, and December 31, 2019, and the most recent 10 years of service are in the School or DPS Divisions	N/A	N/A	PERA 7
PERA	Between January 1, 2017, and December 31, 2019	N/A	N/A	PERA 8
PERA	On or after January 1, 2020	N/A	N/A	PERA 9
DPS	On or before June 30, 2005	Yes	Eligible January 1, 2011	DPS 1
DPS	Between July 1, 2005, and December 31, 2009	Yes	Eligible January 1, 2011	DPS 2
DPS	On or before December 31, 2009	Yes	Not eligible January 1, 2011	DPS 3
DPS	On or before December 31, 2009	No	N/A	DPS 4
Safety Officers	On or before December 31, 2019	N/A	Eligible January 1, 2011	Safety Officers 1
Safety Officers	On or before December 31, 2019	N/A	Not eligible January 1, 2011	Safety Officers 2
Safety Officers	On or after January 1, 2020	N/A	N/A	Safety Officers 3

Once you determine which table applies to you, it's important to look at the table itself as that determines at what combination of years of service and your age you are eligible to retire with either full retirement benefits (the white shaded areas) or reduced retirement benefits (early retirement, the green shaded areas). Note that the blank white areas are combinations of years of service and age where you are not eligible for a retirement benefit at all. If you were to cease working then, you would have to wait until you aged into the green or white shaded areas to receive a benefit from PERA.

As an example, let's look at **Table 9**, which applies to **PERA members hired after January 1, 2020** (this is the latest table and reflects the retirement structure under PERA with the "worst" benefits).

PERA 9

PERA Benefit Structure
Highest Average Salary Percentages
for Retirement Benefit Option 1

Use this table if you began PERA membership on or after January 1, 2020.

Years of Service	Age at Retirement															
	50	51	52	53	54	55	56	57	58	59	60	61	62	63	64	65+
5											7.9	8.6	9.5	10.4	11.4	12.5
6											9.5	10.4	11.4	12.4	13.7	15.0
7											11.1	12.1	13.2	14.5	15.9	17.5
8											12.7	13.8	15.1	16.6	18.2	20.0
9											14.2	15.6	17.0	18.7	20.5	22.5
10											15.8	17.3	18.9	20.7	22.8	25.0
11				No retirement benefits payable.							17.4	19.0	20.8	22.8	25.0	27.5
12											19.0	20.8	22.7	24.9	27.3	30.0
13											20.6	22.5	24.6	27.0	29.6	32.5
14											22.2	24.2	26.5	29.0	31.9	35.0
15											23.7	25.9	28.4	31.1	34.1	37.5
16											25.3	27.7	30.3	33.2	36.4	40.0
17											26.9	29.4	32.2	35.3	38.7	42.5
18											28.5	31.1	34.1	37.3	41.0	45.0
19											30.1	32.9	36.0	39.4	43.2	47.5
20											31.6	34.6	37.9	41.5	45.5	50.0
21											33.2	36.3	39.7	43.5	47.8	52.5
22											34.8	38.1	41.6	45.6	50.1	55.0
23											36.4	39.8	43.5	47.7	52.3	57.5
24											38.0	41.5	45.4	49.8	54.6	60.0
25						28.3	30.8	33.5	36.5	39.8	41.5	43.2	47.3	51.8	56.9	62.5
26						29.4	32.0	34.8	38.0	41.4	45.2	47.2	49.2	53.9	59.2	65.0
27						33.5	33.2	36.2	39.4	43.0	46.9	51.3	53.6	56.0	61.4	67.5
28						38.1	37.8	37.5	40.9	44.6	48.7	53.2	58.2	60.9	63.7	70.0
29						43.2	42.9	42.6	42.3	46.2	50.4	55.1	60.3	66.1	69.2	72.5
30						48.8	48.6	48.3	48.1	47.8	52.2	57.0	62.4	68.4	75.0	75.0
31						55.1	54.9	54.7	54.4	54.2	53.9	58.9	64.5	70.6	77.5	77.5
32						62.0	61.8	61.7	61.5	61.3	61.0	60.8	66.5	72.9	80.0	80.0
33						69.7	69.5	69.4	69.3	69.1	69.0	68.8	68.6	75.2	82.5	82.5
34						78.1	78.1	78.0	77.9	77.9	77.8	77.7	77.6	77.5	85.0	85.0
35	87.5	87.5	87.5	87.5	87.5	87.5	87.5	87.5	87.5	87.5	87.5	87.5	87.5	87.5	87.5	87.5

The shaded areas indicate reduced retirement percentages. These percentages ensure that, as of your effective date of retirement, your reduced retirement benefit is the actuarial equivalent of your full service retirement benefit. These percentages are subject to change based on actuarial experience.

For 35+ years, add 2.5% to 87.5 for each year over 35 up to 100%. Final calculations are made to the exact amount of service you earn, not necessarily even years.

Effective January 1, 2020

The general formula for your defined benefit is **2.5% of your HAS times the number of years of service** you have earned. (Note that in some rare cases, there is a "money purchase" option that might be higher than this calculation. You get whichever is greater.) So, for example, if you have 30 years of service you would be eligible for 75% of your HAS. But there are **minimum age and service requirements** to receive a benefit that are based on your **date of hire** (which is why you have to find the correct table that applies to you.) Once you retire, your benefit is "fixed" at that amount and can only increase by any cost of living adjustment (discussed later).

Let's assume you are age 58, using Table 9, and considering retiring. If you have less than 25 years of service, you would not be eligible for a retirement benefit yet (you're in the blank white area). If you had 20 years of service and retired, you would receive no benefit for two years until you were age 60, at which point you would've "aged" into a reduced retirement benefit of 31.6% of your HAS.

If, instead, you were age 58 and had between 25 and 34 years of service, you would be in the green area and eligible for a reduced retirement benefit starting immediately, ranging from 36.5% to 77.9% of your HAS.

If you had 35 or more years of service, you would be eligible for a full retirement benefit, which is equal to 2.5% times the number of years of service (so between 87.5% and 100% of your HAS - 100% is the maximum you can receive no matter how many years of service you have).

> **Note**: If you are using a table other than Table 9, the rules are different, so make sure you are looking at the correct table applicable to you.

Highest Average Salary (HAS) Calculation
Your defined benefit is calculated as a percentage of your **Highest**

Average Salary (**HAS**), but it's important to understand how your HAS is calculated. Your HAS is calculated by averaging several years of your highest salary, where a "year" is defined as **12 consecutive months**. The number of years you use depends on whether you have **five years of service credit by January 1, 2020**. If you **do**, then your HAS is calculated on your **highest three years**. If **not**, it's your **highest five years**. (Note that the three or five years do not have to be consecutive, it's the three or five highest consecutive 12-month periods.) For most PERA members (but not all), this translates into your last three or five years of service.

But there's a second piece to consider, which is how PERA calculates the salary that your HAS is based on. This also varies by your membership date in (at least) one important way. For members **whose membership date is prior to June 30, 2019**, money placed in a **Section 125 Flexible Spending Account** (other than a Health Savings Account) **comes out pre-PERA**, which means you don't make PERA contributions on it (which is good for you, because your take home pay is higher) but it's not included in your HAS calculation (which is bad for you, but you can adjust **by dropping the Section 125 contributions during your last 3-5 years**, which is the only time it's bad for you).

What are Section 125 contributions? They include any **health, dental and vision insurance premiums** that you pay with pre-tax dollars (often referred to as POP - Premium Only Plans), contributions to **Dependent Care Spending Accounts** (for day care expenses), contributions to **Flexible Spending Accounts** (FSAs, for medical and dental expenses), and contributions to **Limited Purpose FSAs** (for dental and vision only, not medical). (Note that Health Savings Account (HSA) contributions are **not** pre-PERA, but are pre-tax).

Why is this important? Because this is a huge savings for many people because all of those above items (if your membership date is before June 30, 2019) come out pre-PERA, which means you don't pay the current 10.5% (soon to be 11%) PERA contribution on those amounts. This can easily amount to thousands of dollars a year "extra" that you are able to take home instead of contributing to PERA. But when you approach the end of your career, you will want to try to maximize your HAS, which is why many school district remind you to stop doing those things (taking out insurance premiums pre-tax, or contributing to Dependent Care, FSAs or Limited Purpose FSAs) in your last 3-5 years. That will have a short-term negative impact (you will contribute more to PERA and you will pay more in federal and state income taxes because those are not coming out pre-tax), but you will increase your defined benefit for the rest of your life (because the salary your HAS is based on will be much higher). In effect, you work most of your career as if your salary was lower (because PERA only "sees" the after Section 125 amount) and then contribute the "correct" amount for the last few years. (Note that this also saves your employer money, as their contribution is also reduced by your Section 125 contributions.)

Note that there's nothing untoward or unethical about this, this has always been the way the plan was designed. But because of the plan's underfunded status, the legislature made a change in 2018 so that those with a membership date **after June 30, 2019** will **still make PERA contributions on Section 125 contributions** (as will your employer). The "good" news if you will is that for these members, when they reach their final five years they **won't** need to stop using Section 125 plans as they won't affect their HAS (which means they'll still get the federal and state tax breaks those last 3-5 years).

Cost of Living Adjustment (COLA, or AI - Annual Increase)
The last area related to your membership date and your Defined Benefit relates to your annual cost of living adjustment (COLA, but called an **Annual Increase** or **AI** by PERA). When you retire your benefit amount is determined by the formula described in the previous section. That amount is your base retirement benefit and always stays the same but, **after a three-year waiting period**,

it is eligible for an **Annual Adjustment (AI)**. This is designed to help you deal with inflation, as the cost of things still continues to increase over time even though your benefit is static. The cost of living adjustment is currently 1.25%, but can change based on the automatic adjustment provision and can go as low as 0.5% or as high as 2%. The AI will decrease to 1% on July 1, 2022, as a result of the automatic adjustment provision kicking in. These increases are compounded, so each subsequent AI is calculated on your current benefit which includes all previous AIs.

But there is a slight wrinkle to this formula, which is that for those with a **membership date after July 1, 2007**, the AI is the **lesser** of the 1.25% (or whatever the current amount is) or the CPI-W (Consumer Price Index for Urban Wage Earners) for the previous year, and cannot exceed 10% of the **automatic adjustment reserve** set aside for these employees. At this time, neither of those provisions affects the amount, so it's the same no matter your membership date. But there is the possibility in the future that the increase could be smaller for those with a membership date after July 1, 2007 than for those before. (Note: If you retire with a **reduced retirement benefit** you will only get the AI **once you reach the full-retirement age** in your HAS table, **or age 60**, whichever comes first).

Retirement Benefit Options (Option 1, 2 or 3)

Once your retirement benefit is determined according to the rules we just discussed, you then have one more decision to make that affects how much you get each month: which option to take. The options differ based on the death benefit your beneficiary receives when you die

Option 1 is the amount that is calculated according to the rules as discussed. This option provides you with a lifetime monthly benefit. If you die with any remaining balance in your DB Plan account (meaning the benefits that have been paid out have not exceeded your contributions - this usually only happens if you die relatively soon after retiring), a single payment of any remaining balance in your account plus a 100% match on the balance will be made to your named beneficiary or your estate if no named beneficiary exists. There will be no further monthly benefits.

Option 2 pays you a lifetime monthly benefit that is **lower** than your Option 1 benefit but, when you die, your co-beneficiary (typically, but not always, your spouse - it's up to you) **will continue to receive a lifetime monthly benefit equal to 50% of the benefit you were receiving**. How *much* lower your Option 2 benefit is compared to Option 1 is based on an actuarial calculation based on you and your co-beneficiaries ages at the time you retire. (It changes based on current actuarial assumptions, but it's typically between 88% and 98% of your Option 1 benefit, and most likely between 91% and 95%.) If your co-beneficiary dies before you, then your benefit steps back up to your Option 1 level. If your co-beneficiary dies after you and there is still any money left in your DB Plan account that exceeded your contributions (happens infrequently), then that would go to your named beneficiary or your estate.

Option 3 pays you a lifetime monthly benefit that is **lower** than your Option 1 (or Option 2) benefit but, when you die, your co-beneficiary will **continue to receive a lifetime monthly benefit equal to 100% of the benefit you were receiving** (in other words, no change). How much lower your Option 3 benefit is compared to Option 1 is based on an actuarial calculation based on you and your co-beneficiaries ages at the time you retire. (It changes based on current actuarial assumptions, but it's typically between 78% and 96% of your Option 1 benefit, and most likely between 83% and 92%.) If your co-beneficiary dies before you, then your benefit steps back up to your Option 1 level. If your co-beneficiary dies after you and there is still any money left in your DB Plan account that exceeded your contributions (happens infrequently), then that would go to your named beneficiary or your estate.

Which option you (should) choose obviously depends a lot on your individual circumstances, including (but not limited to) your age, your health, whether you have additional retirement savings and/or if you have a spouse who has a retirement benefit or retirement savings. If you are lucky enough to be a two-PERA family, then you have additional considerations as you make this determination. (For what it's worth, my wife and I are a two-PERA family and we both took Option 3, which means the benefits we are currently getting will continue until the second one of us dies, and will actually increase slightly when the first one of us dies.)

Taxes

Your PERA benefit is purchased with pre-tax money (with possibly a partial exception for years you purchase if you purchase them with after-tax money, more on that later), so therefore when you receive your benefit it is considered taxable income. This income is fully taxable but is not considered "earned income", therefore you can't shelter any of it by contributing to a 401k/403b/457/IRA/etc.

Because it's difficult to forecast the tax rates that will be in effect when you retire, planning for this can be very tricky. Just keep in mind that if you anticipate a decent PERA benefit you will likely end up in a "medium" tax bracket, so that may affect other decisions you make like contributing to a traditional vs. a Roth IRA/401k/403b/457.

2.3: DISABILITY AND SURVIVOR BENEFITS

TL;DR: An underappreciated aspect of your PERA benefits is the disability and survivor benefits.

Survivor benefits are just what they sound like, benefits that your survivors receive if you die before retiring. The rules around this are complicated enough that I won't try to summarize them here. Instead, please download PERA's **Survivor Benefits booklet (publication 5-9.pdf** as of this writing). But, briefly, if you die before retirement, your survivors may be eligible for either a lump-sum payment or a monthly benefit. How much that benefit is depends a lot on your age and years of service, whether you were eligible for retirement at your time of death, and the type of survivor (co-beneficiary, spouse, adult children, minor children, etc. - hence why you should download and read the booklet). The main takeaway you should have (at least before reading the booklet) is that if you die before retirement, your survivors will at least get something (your PERA benefit is not "lost") and may indeed get a very nice benefit.

Disability benefits are what you get if you become disabled while working for a PERA employer. An important caveat is that you only qualify for disability benefits once you have **five years of earned service credit** (before that the only disability you might be eligible for would be through your employer if they offer it). Once you have five years of earned service credit, there are two types of disability benefits you can receive: **short-term disability (STD)** or **Disability Retirement**.

If you qualify for **short-term disability** (STD), you can receive up to 22 months of benefits, with a maximum benefit of 60% of your pre-disability income (this can be reduced by a variety of other income replacement programs you may receive from elsewhere). **You must apply within 90 days of stopping working to receive these benefits.** When you apply for disability, your application is evaluated and the third-party administrator determines if you qualify for short-term disability, disability retirement, or don't qualify at all.

If it is determined that you permanently cannot engage in any "regular and substantial gainful employment", you can receive a **disability retirement**. This is a monthly benefit that will continue for as long as you remain disabled (and for your entire life if you are permanently disabled). Again, how much you receive can be complicated, so I recommend you download the **Disability Program Booklet (publication 5-12.pdf** as of this writing). But, briefly, if you have less than 20 years of service you will receive 2.5% of your HAS multiplied by your years of service, plus projected years of service to either 20 years or age 65, whichever is earlier. If you have more than 20 years of service, you will receive 2.5% of HAS multiplied by your years of service. You have the same three options (Option 1, 2 or 3) that you have with a regular retirement.

Note that both survivor and disability benefits are built into PERA, there is no "extra charge" for this benefit.

2.4: PERAPLUS 401(K) AND 457 PLANS

TL;DR: PERA's 401k and 457 Plans - in both Traditional and Roth versions - offer excellent ways to save additional money for your retirement

PERA also offers a voluntary retirement savings plan through its **PERAPlus** 401(k) and 457 plans. Every public school district in Colorado has to offer the PERA 401(k) plan, but they have to opt-in to the 457 plan (many districts have - if your district hasn't, encourage them to do so).

As discussed in Part 1, 401k's are voluntary retirement savings plans offered through many private employers, and sometimes the employer will match some of your contribution. Public employees typically don't have access to a 401k, instead they have access to a 403b and sometimes a 457 plan. PERA's 401k plan was grandfathered, so all public school employees in Colorado definitely have access to it. Many districts also offer 403b plans (the public employee equivalent of a 401k plan) through outside vendors. It's important to know that the 401k and 403b use the same "bucket" of money, meaning the yearly limits that apply to a 401k and 403b are combined for a public employee, not additive. As an example, in 2022 the total you can contribute to a 401k or a 403b if you are under age 50 is $20,500. Even though you can have both a 401k and a 403b as a public school employee in Colorado, the combined amount you can contribute in a calendar year is still $20,500. (Note that if you are over age 50, you can contribute an additional $6,500 so a total of $27,000. These amounts can change each year based on IRS formulas, typically going up by $500 at a time, but not every year.)

In contrast, the 457 plan is a separate "bucket", meaning you can contribute a total of $20,500 to a 401k/403b and an *additional* $20,500 to a 457 plan in the same calendar year. While most public employees don't have enough disposable income to do that, if you have a spouse who makes a lot of money, or if you are doing a transition year with PERA, you might be able to take advantage of this.

It depends on what other vendors and plans your school district offers but, **in general**, PERA's plans are better than the other ones out there. They offer **diversified investments with low fees**, fees that are typically lower than those outside vendors. Assuming you don't have enough disposable income to do both, a logical question is whether to contribute to a 401k (or 403b) or a 457 plan. 457's are very similar to 401k/403b's, but have two significant differences that do make them more attractive all else being equal (meaning there is no difference in investment choices or fees, which is the case with PERA's plans). First, if you leave your employer and withdraw funds before age 59.5, you will not pay a penalty (this is generally not true with 401k/403b's). Second, 457 plans have a special catch-up contribution option where in your final three years of employment you can contribute up to twice the annual amount (so $41,000 instead of $20,500). Again, most folks won't have the income to take advantage of that, but for those who do, it's a nice option.

Both PERA's 401k and 457 plan offer **traditional plans** (pre-tax contributions, so you don't pay tax now, but you pay tax on withdrawals) and **Roth plans** (post-tax contributions, so you do pay taxes on those amounts now, but you don't pay tax when you withdraw contributions and earnings in the future). Depending on your circumstances, you may want to contribute to a traditional, a Roth, or a combination of the two (again, the $20,500/$27,000 combined limit is also a combined limit for the traditional and the Roth, but keep in mind that these contributions do not affect any Traditional or Roth IRA contributions you might make on your own outside of your employment).

To contribute to PERA's 401k or 457 plan, you typically fill out a form (either online or on paper) with your school district (or sometimes with PERA itself for the 457 plan), indicating which plan you are contributing to and how much you want to come out of your paycheck each month (either by dollar amount or by percent). If you reach your annual limit before the end of the year, your district's software should be smart enough to keep you from going over, but it's good to pay attention and make adjustments if necessary (you can change the amount/percentage any given month).

You can find the fees and investment choices for PERA's plans by following the links from their website (currently find them at **copera.org/peraplus-401-k-457-plans**). PERA offers a "white-label" approach, where instead of a long list of mutual funds or ETFs to choose from, they have pre-selected funds for various asset classes (like large cap, small/mid cap, international, real-estate, etc.) Research has shown that it's your asset allocation, not the individual investments you choose, that make the most difference to your long-term return. Also, by doing this, PERA is able to keep management fees low, which allows you to earn a greater return. They also offer Target Date funds or, if you wish, you can utilize a self-directed brokerage account through TD Ameritrade and pick your own investments.

2.5: VOLUNTARY LIFE INSURANCE PLAN

TL;DR: You can likely get better life insurance coverage outside of PERA, but PERA does offer decent life insurance that you are guaranteed to be accepted for.

PERA also offers a voluntary **decreasing term life insurance** plan, where active employees (not inactive or retired members) are guaranteed eligible to enroll (no health questions required) during open enrollment each year. If you enroll while active, you can then continue your enrollment after you retire. There are four tiers of coverage. They currently start at $100,000, $200,000, $300,00 and $400,000 when under age 25, doubled for covered accidents, and coverage decreases with age in age bands, with small benefits for spouse and children, each with a fixed monthly premium, although the premium does increase once you retire if you choose to retain coverage. Your coverage decreases as you get older (in age bands), but your premium remains fixed (except there is a one-time increase when you retire if you decide to keep your life insurance at that point). See PERA's Life Insurance brochure for all the details.

How much coverage can I get?

Tier 1
Active member: $7.75 per month
Retiree: $10.23 per month

Member's Age	Member	Spouse	Child
Less than 25	$100,000	$6,000	Less than
25 – 29	95,000	6,000	14 days — $1,000
30 – 34	85,000	6,000	14 days through age
35 – 39	70,000	6,000	20 — $2,500
40 – 44	40,000	6,000	
45 – 49	30,000	6,000	
50 – 54	20,000	6,000	
55 – 59	15,000	3,500	
60 – 64	7,500	2,500	
65 – 69	5,000	2,500	
70 – 74	3,500	1,000	
75 – 79	2,500	1,000	
80 – 84	2,250	1,000	
85 – 89	1,875	1,000	
90 – 94	1,875	1,000	
95+	1,750	1,000	

Tier 2
Active member: $15.50 per month
Retiree: $20.56 per month

Member's Age	Member	Spouse	Child
Less than 25	$200,000	$12,000	Less than
25 – 29	190,000	12,000	14 days — $2,000
30 – 34	170,000	12,000	14 days through age
35 – 39	140,000	12,000	20 — $5,000
40 – 44	80,000	12,000	
45 – 49	60,000	12,000	
50 – 54	40,000	12,000	
55 – 59	30,000	7,000	
60 – 64	15,000	5,000	
65 – 69	10,000	5,000	
70 – 74	7,000	2,000	
75 – 79	5,000	2,000	
80 – 84	4,500	2,000	
85 – 89	3,750	2,000	
90 – 94	3,750	2,000	
95+	3,500	2,000	

Tier 3
Active member: $23.25 per month
Retiree: $30.84 per month

Member's Age	Member	Spouse	Child
Less than 25	$300,000	$18,000	Less than
25 – 29	285,000	18,000	14 days — $3,000
30 – 34	255,000	18,000	14 days through age
35 – 39	210,000	18,000	20 — $7,500
40 – 44	120,000	18,000	
45 – 49	90,000	18,000	
50 – 54	60,000	18,000	
55 – 59	45,000	10,500	
60 – 64	22,500	7,500	
65 – 69	15,000	7,500	
70 – 74	10,500	3,000	
75 – 79	7,500	3,000	
80 – 84	6,750	3,000	
85 – 89	5,625	3,000	
90 – 94	5,625	3,000	
95+	5,250	3,000	

Tier 4
Active member: $31.00 per month
Retiree: $41.12 per month

Member's Age	Member	Spouse	Child
Less than 25	$400,000	$24,000	Less than
25 – 29	380,000	24,000	14 days — $4,000
30 – 34	340,000	24,000	14 days through age
35 – 39	280,000	24,000	20 — $10,000
40 – 44	160,000	24,000	
45 – 49	120,000	24,000	
50 – 54	80,000	24,000	
55 – 59	60,000	14,000	
60 – 64	30,000	10,000	
65 – 69	20,000	10,000	
70 – 74	14,000	4,000	
75 – 79	10,000	4,000	
80 – 84	9,000	4,000	
85 – 89	7,500	4,000	
90 – 94	7,500	4,000	
95+	7,000	4,000	

2.6: PERACARE

TL;DR: Health insurance (and, to a lesser extent, dental and vision insurance) is a huge concern after you retire. PERACare offers you guaranteed coverage at decent rates and even provides a small subsidy.

PERACare is PERA's health benefits program for retirees and benefit recipients, which includes health, dental, and vision care programs. You may be enrolled in any or all three types of coverage, and you may also enroll your eligible dependents in any of the plans in which you participate. You can enroll when you retire and (presumably) lose your employer-sponsored coverage, or each year during the open enrollment period.

If you are under age 65, then PERA offers **Pre-Medicare** from several vendors. Once you turn 65, then PERA offers (or switches you over to) **Medicare** coverage available from several vendors. These are group policies that you are **guaranteed eligible for**, but are optional. You may have better options available through a spouse or through the open insurance marketplace.

While these policies are not inexpensive, they are typical of group insurance costs and can leverage the size of PERA to get better rates. You are also guaranteed to be accepted, which is a big deal as you get older. Having said that, you are part of an older group with PERACare, so therefore rates can be higher and you may be able to find better rates elsewhere (see **fischfinancial.org/2021/06/18/health-insurance-peracare-vs-the-aca-marketplace/** for more).

In order to help with affordability, PERA helps subsidize the cost of your health insurance, prorated on the number of years of service you retire with. For Pre-Medicare plans, you can get a subsidy of up to $230 a month, and for Medicare plans up to $115 a month (because Medicare plans are so much less expensive). The subsidy is prorated per year of service up to year 20, which is when you get the full subsidy. Your PERACare premiums - minus the subsidy - will be automatically deducted from your benefit check each month.

2.7: PURCHASING
SERVICE CREDIT

TL;DR: Many PERA members are unaware that they can purchase additional years in PERA, based on non-PERA covered employment, which can increase their defined benefit amount and perhaps allow them to retire earlier.

Many PERA members don't realize that they may be eligible to **purchase years of service credit**. This idea might be counterintuitive, but the idea is that if you've worked for a while in non-PERA-covered employment, this is an opportunity to "buy" those years into PERA. Once the years are bought, they act just like years you've worked for a PERA employer, which means that you will have more years that your defined benefit is based on, you may be able to retire earlier, and it may boost your PERACare subsidy amount.

When and how many years you can purchase depends both on your membership date and the details of your outside work experience. If your membership date is **before January 1, 1999,** you must have **one year** of earned service credit and then you are eligible to **purchase up to 10 years of combined qualified or nonqualified employment** (defined below). If your membership date is **after January 1, 1999,** you must have **one year of earned service credit to purchase qualified employment** and **five years of earned service credit to purchase nonqualified employment,** and you can purchase up to **five years** of nonqualified employment and up to **ten years** total.

Download the **Purchasing Service Credit brochure** (**publication 5-52.pdf** as of this writing) for all the details, but **qualified employment** is any U.S. employment where the employer is set up under federal, state, or local government, as well as public and private K-12 school employment, and employment with public employee organizations, such as CAPE, CEA, etc, including time with a PERA-covered employer where you were considered an exempt employee (for example, working part-time at a state university in Colorado while going to school).

Nonqualified employment is all employment which does not fit into qualified employment and basically includes any non-PERA covered employment in the private sector or in a foreign country. (This is simplified a bit, so check out the brochure or contact PERA to clarify if necessary.)

You do not have to purchase service credit in whole year increments, you can purchase by months or even partial months. For any month to qualify for purchase, you must have made **80 times the minimum wage in effect during that month** in order to purchase a full month of credit. For example, right now the federal minimum wage in effect is $7.25 an hour, so for any employment right now, you'd have to make $580 to be eligible to purchase a full month of service credit. (In the past when the minimum wage was lower, the monthly amount would've been lower as well.) Many people will have months or even years where they worked before being covered by PERA employment, even part-time during high school and college, that could qualify for purchasing service credit. PERA will help you determine what you are eligible to purchase, you just provide documentation of your earnings (pay stubs, tax returns, or social security earnings statements available at **ssa.gov/myaccount**).

Purchasing service credit is often not cheap, as the cost to purchase service credit is the actuarial cost of providing the future benefit resulting from the purchase and is calculated using your HAS, your age, and your PERA membership start date. Having said that, this is often a great option for many educators, especially early in their career when their HAS is not very high (assuming, of course, that you have the money to make the purchase).

For many people, the ideal way to purchase these years is with **pre-tax** money, from your 401k/403b/457 plan. You can, however, use **post-tax** money (any savings or investments you have). If you use post-tax money, the portion of your benefit that you end up receiving that is from this part of your purchase will be post-tax, so will not be subject to taxes when you receive it.

The decision around purchasing is complicated and varies tremendously, but basically the tradeoff you are making is **trading a chunk of money now** (that you could possibly invest and make a lot of money with over time) for a **guaranteed increased monthly income for life**. For many people, that is a great tradeoff to make (especially if you choose Option 2 or 3, so it's increased income for life for the combined life expectancy of you and your co-beneficiary). Also keep in mind the benefit of possibly retiring earlier (as it moves you into the green reduced retirement range and the white full retirement age at an earlier age than if you didn't purchase service credit), and can increase your PERACare subsidy if you would normally have been retiring with less than 20 years of service.

PERA counselors are very helpful at not only helping you figure out how many years you can purchase and what the cost would be, but at helping you evaluate the pros and cons of purchasing. The great thing about PERA is that they are not trying to sell you anything, they get paid for giving good service, so their advice is not compromised by financial incentives to sell you something. I think everyone should at least explore purchasing service credit and get the details, even if you end up deciding not to purchase.

2.8: WORKING AFTER RETIREMENT

TL;DR: Once you retire and begin receiving a PERA benefit, you can return to work, but there are limitations if you return to a PERA-covered-employer.

Once you are receiving a PERA retirement benefit, some members may choose to return to work. If you return to work with a non-PERA-covered employer, there are no restrictions on how much you can work and how much you can earn - your PERA benefit will be unaffected.

But if you return to work with a PERA-covered employer, it's a bit more complicated.

- You must not work during the month of your effective retirement, or your benefit will be reduced.

- If you return to work for a PERA employer and are not an independent contractor, you are limited to 110 days or 720 hours of work per calendar year. If you exceed those limits, PERA will reduce your benefit. If you are an independent contractor, you are not subject to those limits. You (and your employer) will still make PERA contributions, but you will not earn additional service credit.

See the Working After Retirement brochure (**publication 2-55.pdf** as of this writing) for more details.

Note that while many retirees don't want to return to work, this is a nice option if the financial necessity arises. Also keep in mind that the 110 day/720 hour calendar year limit allows for something called a **"transition year"** that allows you to retire with PERA (and start receiving your PERA benefit) and still work one more year with your PERA employer. We will discuss this more in Part 3.

2.9: PERA SUMMARY

TL;DR: Knowledge (of your PERA benefits) is power.

These are the highlights of your PERA benefits, but in a book of this length I can't cover everything. So be sure to explore the PERA website or meet with a PERA counselor to get more or to clarify information. PERA is an unusual organization in many ways, one of the most prominent of which is how focused they are on customer service. They don't have to try to sell you anything, so their entire goal when working with you is to help you make better informed decisions. So don't hesitate to reach out to them via phone or an in-person (or virtual) visit, to ask anything from seemingly "simple" to very complex questions.

Many folks are unaware of all the benefits that PERA offers and the degree to which these benefits should influence the rest of your financial decisions. Part 3 will take a look at several of the financial areas from Part 1 and show you how your PERA benefits - in conjunction with your school district benefits - will likely change how you approach some of those decisions in order to optimize your finances.

PART 3: HOW TO OPTIMIZE YOUR FINANCIAL PLANNING TO TAKE ADVANTAGE OF PERA AND YOUR SCHOOL DISTRICT BENEFITS

This part focuses on how your PERA benefits - along with the other benefits from your school district - impact almost all of the financial areas discussed in Part 1, and how you can optimize those decisions based on those benefits.

3.1: OPTIMIZING YOUR DEFINED BENEFIT

TL;DR: Now that you know more about how your defined benefit is calculated, here are some ways to optimize it.

There are three (at least) ways to optimize the defined benefit you will ultimately receive from PERA.

Purchase Service Credit
As discussed previously, for every year of service credit you purchase, you get an additional 2.5% of your HAS (or prorated for partial years). So, as an example, if you can purchase 6 years of service credit (like I did), you will increase your (Option 1) benefit amount by 15%. That also may allow you to retire earlier with either reduced or full retirement benefits. This not only gives you a bigger "paycheck" in retirement, but gives you much appreciated flexibility on when you can retire. Also keep in mind that if you choose Option 2 or 3, the impact would be less than 15% but would apply to the joint life expectancy of you and your co-beneficiary. (If you are a two-PERA family like we are, and you both can purchase 6 years like we did, it's fantastic in many, many ways.)

Maximize Your PERA-Includable Salary in Your HAS Years
There are two ways (at least) to do this.

First, if your membership date is **before June 30, 2019**, be sure to **stop** paying insurance premiums pre-tax and contributing to any

Section 125 plans in **your last 3-5 years of service**. This will lower your take home pay a bit for those years, but will maximize the salary that your HAS is calculated on. (If your membership date is after that, you do **not** need to stop because your Section 125 contributions are not coming out pre-PERA.)

Second, the years that your HAS is calculated on are a great time to earn any extra money from your school district that might be available to you (life circumstances and energy level permitting). This can include anything from changing positions (from teacher to instructional coach or administrator for example), to taking on extra duties (coaching, Department Chair, mentoring), to working taking tickets or supervising athletic events or activities. You obviously have to evaluate if the money is worth your time, but keep in mind that not only are you earning those extra dollars for 3-5 years, but you will be getting a larger check for hopefully 30+ years in retirement. (See **bit.ly/salaryschedulelanes** for more)

Insurance and Other School District Benefits
As discussed previously, for those with a membership date **before June 30, 2019**, any insurance premiums or Section 125 contributions you can make pre-tax will give you a "bonus" of 10.5% (soon to be 11%) in contributions you won't be making to PERA (again, be sure to stop this in your last 3-5 years). Be sure to take advantage of all the Section 125 options that you can during this time, including FSA's and Limited Purpose FSA's if you have them, and Dependent Care Spending Accounts if you have children who need day care. (Many folks don't realize that utilizing the Dependent Care Spending Account works out to a daycare discount of around 37% for most educators, at least up to the $5,000 maximum you can currently contribute.) But then be sure to stop all of these in your last 3-5 years to maximize your HAS.

Also, most school districts in Colorado offer access to a High Deductible Health Insurance Plan. As discussed in Part 1, many people are scared away from these plans because of the high deductible but, when you do the math, they are often cheaper than the non-high-deductible plans (and significantly cheaper during healthy years). This is due to a combination of you paying lower premiums and your district often contributing money to your HSA. If you can afford to max out your HSA each year and **not** spend from it (pay for any medical expenses out of pocket instead of from your HSA), you can also invest it and let it grow for the long term. We'll talk more about this later when we talk about how PERA lets you optimize your investments.

Most school districts offer employees at least some life insurance. Be sure to take that amount into account when considering whether to purchase PERA's life insurance (and when deciding how much to purchase), and also be sure to get quotes from independent agents. Often - but not always - you can get better life insurance outside of PERA (and your employer's optional life insurance offerings), so be sure to compare. Make sure the total amount of life insurance is appropriate for your life situation.

3.2: OPTIMIZE YOUR VOLUNTARY RETIREMENT PLAN AND HSA INVESTMENTS (ASSET ALLOCATION)

TL;DR: Because of your excellent defined benefit through PERA you are able to invest more aggressively throughout your career (and even into retirement) and earn a higher long-term rate of return.

This is a tough one to discuss in a general way, as the "right" decisions will vary tremendously based on your individual circumstances. But everyone should be contributing to a 401k/403b/457 plan and possibly also an IRA outside of work. (And, if you have a High Deductible Health Plan, you should be trying to max out your HSA and invest that for the long term, too.) It's important to compare the offerings from any vendors your district has contracted with to offer 403b's or 457 plans with those that PERA offers (every district must offer PERA's 401k, they can choose to offer PERA's 457), along with what you can invest in in your personal IRA.

A 403b is the public employer equivalent of the 401k, it's an employer-sponsored savings plan for retirement. Public employers also have the option of offering a 457b plan (so you can tax-defer even more money if you are able), which is similar but offers some additional attractive options. The problem with 403b's (and some 457's), is that they often have fees that are way too high. Those fees often end up more than offsetting any tax advantages you get from using those accounts. (See **bit.ly/ tldr403b** for more.)

> If you are comparing your district's 403b/457 offerings to the offerings from PERA, you need to pay careful attention to the fees and investment choices your district vendor(s) offer. PERA's fees will usually be lower, but not always. And the fees you can get with your personal IRA at a place like Vanguard are likely to be the lowest overall. Because each district can (sometimes) negotiate different fees from a vendor, you can't always assume that the fees the vendor offers elsewhere are the same ones you have. Two excellent places to learn more about this are **403bwise.org** and **403bcompare.com**. In **general**, the following vendors are likely to be the only good district-level 403b/457 choices with relatively low fees and good investment choices:
>
> - Aspire
> - Fidelity Investments
> - ICMA-RC
> - TIAA
> - T. Rowe Price
> - Vanguard

Make sure you look for both **administrative fees** and the **individual investment fund expenses** and **combine them before you compare**. I have created a spreadsheet that allows you to compare fees (find it at **fischlearning.com/ scenarios-for-colorado-public-employees/**). Make a copy of the spreadsheet if you want to customize it for your situation. (Also see **bit.ly/fischfeesmatter** for more.)

For many folks (unless you get an employer match), the **best option is to invest in an IRA** (either Traditional or Roth, and preferably through Vanguard or someone similar). You can invest in low-cost, diversified index funds through Vanguard for less than 0.15% expense ratios, which is typically much less than you can through your 403b/457. Keep in mind, however, that there are income limits that might preclude you from investing in an IRA. They change each year, and there are different limits for Traditional vs. Roth, check the IRS website or just google to find the current year limits. Note that any pre-tax deductions to a traditional 401k/403b/457 reduces your income for this calculation, so often by contributing to a Traditional 401k/403b/457, you can lower your AGI enough to qualify to also contribute to an IRA. And, unfortunately, the total amount you can invest in an IRA each year (currently $6,000 if you are under age 50) is lower than what you can invest in a 401k/403b/457 (currently $20,500 if you are under age 50).

Once you've maxed out your personal IRA (assuming your income qualifies), then a 401k/403b/457 is your next good option. Again, check with your district to see what they offer, but most likely PERA's 401k is going to be the better choice. If your district offers PERA's 457, consider that before the 401k (you can do both if you have the ability to save that much from your paycheck). A 457 plan not only gives you an additional "bucket" of tax-deferred investment in addition to the 401k/403b bucket, and it has more liberal withdrawal rules before the age of 59.5. Since the fees are the same for PERA's 401k and 457, you might as well choose the 457 for that additional flexibility.

There are also some tricky calculations to do around whether to contribute to traditional plans or Roth plans. Contributing to traditional plans gets you a tax break now and also lowers your adjusted gross income which can sometimes qualify you for other tax breaks that you might not get if you didn't contribute. But because you are going to get a very good defined benefit (if you work for your PERA employer(s) for a long enough time), and that defined benefit will be fully taxable income when you get it, realize that withdrawals that you ultimately make from a traditional 401k/403b/457 plan will likely be taken at a higher marginal tax rate than you might be expecting. That sometimes can tip the scale in favor of doing a Roth contribution instead. (Since it's often hard to tell for sure, lots of people split their contributions between both to remain flexible based on tax policy in the future.)

Many school districts in Colorado offer access to a High Deductible Health Insurance Plan. As discussed in Part 1, many people are scared away from these plans because of the high deductible but, when you do the math, they are often cheaper than the non-high-deductible plans (and significantly cheaper during healthy years). This is due to a combination of you paying lower premiums and your district often contributing money to your HSA. If you can afford to max out your HSA each year and **not** spend from it (pay for any medical expenses out of pocket instead of from your HSA), you can also invest it and let it grow for the long term.

Your HSA in effect can turn into a **"stealth IRA"**, only even better because this money is never taxed. Note that HSAs are "better" than either Traditional or Roth IRAs because they are **triple-tax advantaged**: contributions, earnings and withdrawals are never taxed as long as you use them for medical expenses (and you can "accumulate" medical expenses over time and reimburse yourself for them in the future). So, if you can afford to pay medical expenses just from your regular cash flow, don't tap into your HSA and just invest it for the long run like you would your 401k/403b/457, and then begin withdrawing it (for medical expenses) in retirement. (See **bit.ly/tldrhsa** for more.)

One more consideration is *how* you invest your money in 401k/403b/457/IRAs/HSA/etc., whether they are traditional or Roth. As discussed in Part 1, many people invest too conservatively for their retirement, not realizing that the long-term nature of their investments makes "aggressive" investments not as risky over the long-term. For PERA members (at least those who anticipate working a full career with a PERA-covered employer), this is even more true. Here's why.

Your PERA Defined Benefit is **guaranteed income for life**, with a (modest) cost of living adjustment built in. As a result, this functions very much like the bond (fixed income) portion of your portfolio. Using the 4% rule of thumb (not really a "rule", but a good way to approximate), take your anticipated yearly defined benefit amount and multiply by 25. (If both you and your spouse have defined benefit plans and/or Social Security, do that for your combined amounts.)

For example, let's say you anticipate your yearly defined benefit to be $80,000 (not that unrealistic for a career teacher retiring in 2030, for example). If you multiply that by 25, that's the rough "equivalent" of $2 million invested in bonds (4% of $2 million is $80,000 a year). To be clear, it's a "rough equivalent". On the negative side, when you (or your co-beneficiary) dies, the $80,000 a year stops, whereas if there's anything left in your bond portfolio that could be left to your heirs. But on the positive side, the $80,000 a year continues for your (joint) life expectancy, whereas if you spend down your bond portfolio to $0, not only will nothing be left for your heirs, but you'll be eating ramen noodles three times a day. (Another good way to think about a defined benefit is as **longevity insurance** - you can't outlive it, although eventually inflation will take its toll).

So if you're expecting a decent defined benefit, and that translates into the equivalent of a huge investment in fixed income (bonds), then what should you be investing your money in? Your defined benefit (guaranteed income for life) means that your asset allocation - how you divide your investments between stocks (equities), bonds (fixed income) and perhaps other asset classes (real estate, cash, etc.) - can be **much more aggressive**. In general, that means that PERA members can invest more of their portfolio than most people can in "riskier" investments like stocks and less in "safer" investments like bonds. (Note that "riskier" and "safer" are historically a short-term distinction, over longer periods of time stocks have outperformed bonds so therefore might not be considered riskier in the long term.)

Now, to be perfectly clear, this depends on the rest of your financial situation and, crucially, on your **risk tolerance**. While over time stocks are very likely to outperform bonds, and while over time stocks have always gone up, stocks are also much more volatile than bonds and can also go down - and often by a lot (for example, by over 30% in March of 2020 and by about 50% in 2007-2009). So not only do you need to take into account the rest of your financial situation when making this decision, you have to take into account *your own likely behavior* should the stock market drop precipitously. If you suspect (or know) that you would panic and sell your stocks when the market drops that much, then you don't want your asset allocation to be so aggressive. By having more "safer" investments like bonds in your portfolio, you will be more likely (behaviorally) to "ride out" the drop in the market (with the trade off being lower total returns over time).

On the other hand, if you know that you can "ride out the lows", perhaps because you've done it before (2007-2009, or March 2020) or because you know that the mathematics has always worked out in the long run, then you should consider making your asset allocation much more "aggressive" (heavily weighted towards equities). Since your long-term bucket is going to be invested for a long enough period of time that you should be able to ride out the lows, and because you have a defined benefit that you can count on, you should even consider making your retirement investment portfolio 100% equities. That's not a typo, if you have a good defined benefit, you should *consider* making your long-term retirement investments 100% in stocks. (See **bit.ly/tldrtarget** for more.)

Because you will not be completely relying on these investments to live on (because of your defined benefit), you won't find yourself in the situation of "spending down" your investments too quickly if you happen to retire during a bear (down) market. You can simply cut down on some of your "extra", discretionary spending until the market recovers. For example, perhaps you travel less if the market happens to be way down just after you retire, and then start travelling more once it recovers. On the other hand, if the market is not down a lot right after you retire, you are likely to have a lot more available to spend because you've invested more aggressively (and then you can just cut back some in the future should the markets drop a lot later).

I want to be perfectly clear here, this is a decision you need to **think about carefully**. There is no "one size fits all" advice that is going to apply to everyone. But many folks want to be told some specifics, so I'll do my best. So, if you have a good defined benefit (and especially if you are a two-PERA family with two good defined benefits) here is one way to perhaps help you decide where you fall based on your risk tolerance.

High Risk Tolerance: *"Even if my retirement portfolio were to drop by 50% like it would have in 2007-2009, I would still ride it out and not sell my stocks at the bottom of the market."*

> If you truly think the above is true, either because you had a significant portfolio in 2007-2009 and you didn't sell or because you are very, very confident you would not if (when) this happens again, then you have a high risk tolerance and you should *consider* investing in 100% equities in your retirement portion of your portfolio. Here's what that might look like in PERA's 401k/457 plan, in your Traditional or Roth IRA at Vanguard, and in a 403b/457 at a vendor other than PERA (these are just examples, with expense ratios noted in parenthesis).

PERA 401k/457 (Fees include $12 a year for the account plus the expense ratio for each fund below)
40% PERAdvantage U.S. Large Cap Stock Fund (0.08%)
30% PERAdvantage U.S. Small and Mid Cap Stock Fund (0.18%)
30% PERAdvantage International Stock Fund (0.29%)

Vanguard Traditional and/or Roth IRA
40% Vanguard Total Stock Market Index Fund (VTSAX, 0.04%)
30% Vanguard Small Cap Value Index Fund (VSIAX, 0.07%)
30% Vanguard Total International Stock Index Fund (VTIAX, 0.11%)

Other 403b/457/HSA Vendor
This depends on what the vendor offers, but look for index funds with low expense ratios
40% Total Stock Market Index Fund or S&P 500 Index Fund (varies)
30% Small Cap or Small Cap Value Index Fund (varies)
30% Total International Stock Index Fund (varies)

Rebalancing
Because the three different funds will grow at different rates, you would want to periodically **rebalance** between the three funds to get you back to your original percentages of asset allocation between the funds. This keeps you within your asset allocation and forces you to "sell high(er), buy low(er)". There are two ways to consider doing this.

Easier: Once a year check your portfolio and rebalance back to the original percentages.

Harder (but not hard): Set up percentage bands. For example, a good rule of thumb might be to rebalance any time one of your funds is more than 4% different than your allocation. For example, if your PERAdvantage U.S. Large

Cap Stock Fund grew to more than 44% (or less than 36%) of your total portfolio, then you would rebalance. (Same idea for the other two funds.) While this takes a bit more effort than rebalancing once a year, some research has indicated that you could earn a bit more over time because it can let your "winners run" a bit longer before rebalancing.

Medium Risk Tolerance: *"Even if my retirement portfolio were to drop by 33% like it would have in March of 2020 due to the Covid pandemic, I would still ride it out and not sell my stocks at the bottom of the market."*

If you truly think the above is true, either because you had a significant portfolio in March 2020 and you didn't sell or because you are very, very confident you would not if (when) this happens again, then you have a medium risk tolerance and you should consider investing your retirement portion of your portfolio in such a way that equities are overweighted (but not 100%). Here's what that might look like in PERA's 401k/457 plan, in your Traditional or Roth IRA at Vanguard, and in a 403b/457 at a vendor other than PERA.

PERA 401k/457 (Fees include $12 a year for the account plus the expense ratio for each fund below)
50% PERAdvantage U.S. Large Cap Stock Fund (0.08%)
50% PERAdvantage Target Retirement Date Funds. Pick the fund that is roughly 10 years past the year you anticipate retiring. So if you are anticipating retiring in 2040, pick the 2050 fund. (0.10%)

Vanguard Traditional and/or Roth IRA
50% Vanguard Total Stock Market Index Fund (VTSAX, 0.04%)
50% Vanguard Target Retirement Date Fund. Pick the fund that is roughly 10 years past the year you anticipate

retiring. So if you are anticipating retiring in 2040, pick the 2050 fund. (0.15%)

Other 403b/457/HSA Vendor

This depends on what the vendor offers, but look for index funds with low expense ratios

50% Total Stock Market Index Fund or S&P 500 Index Fund (varies)

50% Target Retirement Date Fund. Pick the fund that is roughly 10 years past the year you anticipate retiring. So if you are anticipating retiring in 2040, pick the 2050 fund. (varies)

Rebalancing

Just as with the High Risk Tolerance, you would want to periodically rebalance using one of the two methods described previously.

Lower Risk Tolerance: *"Even if my retirement portfolio were to drop by 15% like it would have in most years the stock market has been around, I would still ride it out and not sell my stocks at the bottom of the market."*

If you truly think the above is accurate, either because you've had a significant portfolio for a while and you didn't sell when the market periodically corrects, or because you are very, very confident you would not when this happens again (it happens fairly often), then you have a lower risk tolerance and you should consider investing your retirement portion of your portfolio in such a way that equities are overweighted (but not as overweighted as the Medium Risk Tolerance). Here's what that might look like in PERA's 401k/457 plan, in your Traditional or Roth IRA at Vanguard, and in a 403b/457 at a vendor other than PERA.

PERA 401k/457 (Fees include $12 a year for the account plus the expense ratio for each fund below)

25% PERAdvantage U.S. Large Cap Stock Fund (0.08%)
75% PERAdvantage Target Retirement Date Funds. Pick the fund that is roughly 10 years past the year you anticipate retiring. So if you are anticipating retiring in 2040, pick the 2050 fund. (0.10%)

Vanguard Traditional and/or Roth IRA
25% Vanguard Total Stock Market Index Fund (VTSAX, 0.04%)
75% Vanguard Target Retirement Date Fund. Pick the fund that is roughly 10 years past the year you anticipate retiring. So if you are anticipating retiring in 2040, pick the 2050 fund. (0.15%)

Other 403b/457/HSA Vendor
This depends on what the vendor offers, but look for index funds with low expense ratios
25% Total Stock Market Index Fund or S&P 500 Index Fund (varies)
75% Target Retirement Date Fund. Pick the fund that is roughly 10 years past the year you anticipate retiring. So if you are anticipating retiring in 2040, pick the 2050 fund. (varies)

Rebalancing
You would want to periodically rebalance using one of the two methods described previously.

Very Low Risk Tolerance: *"I know that I will likely panic and sell if I check my retirement portfolio occasionally and it has dropped significantly."*

If this applies to you, then you should just pick a Target Date fund and then forget about it. It will rebalance for you and, because you don't have to check your balance, it should be easier to avoid panicking. Here's what that might look like in PERA's 401k/457 plan, in your Traditional or Roth IRA at

Vanguard, and in a 403b/457 at a vendor other than PERA.

PERA 401k/457 (Fees include $12 a year for the account plus the expense ratio for each fund below)
100% PERAdvantage Target Retirement Date Funds. Pick the fund that is roughly 10 years past the year you anticipate retiring. So if you are anticipating retiring in 2040, pick the 2050 fund. (0.10%)

Vanguard Traditional and/or Roth IRA
100% Vanguard Target Retirement Date Fund. Pick the fund that is roughly 10 years past the year you anticipate retiring. So if you are anticipating retiring in 2040, pick the 2050 fund. (0.15%)

Other 403b/457/HSA Vendor
This depends on what the vendor offers, but look for index funds with low expense ratios
100% Target Retirement Date Fund. Pick the fund that is roughly 10 years past the year you anticipate retiring. So if you are anticipating retiring in 2040, pick the 2050 fund. (varies)

Rebalancing
You would **not** need to rebalance because the fund does it for you and you just have the one fund.

"Never" Sell
No matter which risk tolerance you fall under, your strategy (in your long-term bucket) should be to **never sell** (except when you are rebalancing between your existing funds). Once you've picked your strategy, **stick with it until you are retired** and start withdrawing the money. (At that point, you might consider shifting your asset allocation a bit, but that's beyond the scope of this book.)

3.3: TRANSITION YEAR

TL;DR: Some members may want to take advantage of the ability to retire and start receiving their PERA benefit while still working one more year with their employer. This decision is perhaps more complicated than you think.

Because **school years** conveniently break roughly half and half across **two calendar years**, this opens up the possibility of doing a **"transition year."** Note that not every school district offers this option. (Although, as an aside, I don't feel like they should be the ones who get to decide this as your income from a PERA benefit is totally separate from your employment with them. But I digress.)

Since most public school employees choose to retire at the end of the school year, it opens up the opportunity to retire in May (or June), start drawing your retirement benefit, but then continue to work the next school year. If you retire in May (or June), and then don't work in June (or July), then you satisfy PERA's "not working in the month of your retirement" rule for working after retirement. Then when you start working in August, you typically will not work more than 110 days (as a salaried employee) or 720 hours (as an hourly employee) before the end of the calendar year (which is PERA's working after retirement limit in any calendar year). Then a new calendar year starts, and you typically won't work more than 110 days/720 hours during second semester. At the end of the school year, you will then stop working and not run afoul of the working after retirement rules.

Note: There is nothing stopping you from taking a year off and then doing this again - one school year off, then one school year on - and then repeating that pattern multiple times. Some school districts may not allow this so you might have to move districts.

Many folks really like this option, because it's **almost** like getting paid double that last year of work - you get your PERA benefit and your regular paycheck (typically for 14 months). But I say **almost** because it's not really double, it's often somewhere **between 1.25 and 1.75 times** your regular salary. First, your PERA benefit is not going to be equivalent to your salary (unless you have 40 years of service which equates to 100% of your HAS). Second, most (all?) school districts stop paying for your benefits during this transition year, which means you'll have to pay those out of pocket. (Again, as an aside, this doesn't make any sense to me, this should be independent of your PERA retirement and should have no effect on your benefits. But, again, I digress.) Third, many school districts also "freeze" your salary at the end of your last non-transition year, so you forego any yearly raise that you normally would receive by moving one more step on the salary schedule and whatever yearly cost-of-living increase there is to the salary schedule itself. When you take these three factors into account, then your income will definitely be less than double, but will still be higher than if you didn't "retire."

Traditionally, many folks have considered this option a "no brainer", but I would caution you that it is not quite so simple and, for many people, it would be better to **not** take a transition year. As with all things, this very much depends on your personal situation, but let me try to lay out some of the factors you should consider. (In some ways, taking a transition year is the opposite of the decision of purchasing a year of credit. It's not a perfect comparison, but it's a pretty good way to think about it.)

By working a transition year, you have one year where you have a **fairly significant boost in income**, which is a nice way to start off retirement. But what you are giving up - **in addition to paid benefits**, which is pretty significant on its own - is the **additional year of service credit** you would receive if you didn't retire with PERA and start receiving your benefit. That means you are **giving** up an additional **2.5% of your HAS, and** your **HAS would likely be slightly higher** because you would include this year at a presumably higher salary than the year it was "replacing" in your HAS from four (or six) years ago (depending on whether you were vested before January 1, 2020). (One other thing, if you take the transition year and then decide, for whatever reason, that you don't want to retire, that can be problematic. If you just work that last year like normal and then change your mind, nothing changes.)

Many people will try to run a "break even" analysis on this. They'll calculate how much "extra" income they will have if they take the transition year and are working and receiving a PERA benefit, and then they will compare that with the additional benefit they would receive if they didn't take the transition year, and then do the math to try to figure out how long they have to live to "break even" in order figure out which one is "higher." They often will also try to factor in how much they can earn on their investments if they take the "extra" money from the transition year and invest it, which is a legitimate factor to consider, but only if you actually invest that money.

But the problem with this break even analysis (in addition to the fact that most folks forget to subtract out the cost of the benefits they have to pay that last year) is the **behavioral aspect** of this. Yes, if you do the math, and if you take the extra additional income you would make during the transition year and invest it in all equity portfolio, there is a decent chance you will come out "ahead" compared to the increased monthly benefit if you worked one more year and got that additional service credit. But, **psychologically**, for many people it is **much harder to actually spend the money** in their investment portfolio as compared to the monthly benefit check they get from PERA. For many folks, they have spent many years saving and investing and building up their nest egg and then, suddenly, they have to decide how much they are comfortable withdrawing from their investments and spending on something.

You may think that's not you, that you have no trouble spending money. That may be the case, but it's different in retirement because you no longer have an earned income in the future to plan on. And even the most free-spending people have the "what if" concerns, particularly around future medical and long-term care expenses, that often make them hesitant to spend down that nest egg too quickly. No one wants to outlive their money.

On the other hand, the check you get in retirement from PERA each month (as well as your spouse's check from their retirement plan or social security), is something that **you can count on** coming this month, and next month, and the next...**for the rest of your life**. It is much, much, **much** easier to feel comfortable spending that money because you know it will be "replenished" the very next month with another check, and that will go on until your death. (And, with PERA, if you take Option 2 or 3, it will go on until the death of the second one of you.)

So, even though **mathematically** (and assuming what your investment return will be on any invested money is correct) it may be the better bet to take the transition year, **behaviorally** it may not be. You may actually have a **higher standard of living in retirement by not taking the transition year** because you will actually be comfortable spending more money each month, even though (mathematically) you might have more total money by taking the transition year. (On the other hand, if the thing you value the most is leaving an **inheritance** for your heirs, then taking a transition year and investing the extra will likely - but not always - increase the size of that inheritance when compared to not taking the transition year.)

For what it's worth, I did take a transition year and my wife did not. This was partially due to the math calculation and partially due to circumstance. We were able to essentially invest my entire paycheck and my wife's entire paycheck and just live off my PERA benefit during my transition year. Because my wife was still teaching, our daughter and I were able to be on my wife's employer's insurance which, while not cheap, was still less expensive than if we were getting it on our own. My wife was planning on teaching for another year or two, but ended up retiring at the end of the 2019-20 school year due to the pandemic. Because that wasn't "planned", there was no opportunity to take a transition year even if we had wanted to, but most likely we would have chosen not to if we had had the choice (because of the combination of one more year of paid benefits, another year boosting her HAS, and the additional 2.5% of HAS, combined with the behavioral aspects mentioned above.)

Now, I want to be clear, **this doesn't mean that you shouldn't take a transition year**. For many people that will be the decision they will end up making and it will be the right one. But it does mean that you need to **think about this a bit more carefully than perhaps most people have**, and be **very thoughtful and intentional** about your decision.

Transition Year vs. Working One More Year	
Transition Year	**Working One More Year**
• One year of "extra" income that you can choose how you want to spend or invest	• Lifetime of additional monthly income by adding another 2.5% of HAS (longevity insurance)
• Ability to save and invest more and possibly earn higher returns over the long run	• Likely increases HAS for additional boost to monthly income
• Extra income might allow you to "supercharge" your contributions to a 457 plan that you can then more easily withdraw from without penalty if you are retiring before the age of 59.5	• Employer still pays for benefits for that year
	• You still get any raise from moving one more step plus any increase to the salary schedule itself
	• Easier psychologically to spend income you know you will receive each month
• More likely to increase the legacy inheritance you will be able to leave to your heirs	• Shifts the risk from you (through your investment and withdrawal choices) to the state of Colorado (through PERA)
	• Allows you to easily

change your mind about
retiring

- If you are retiring early
(the green area of the HAS
tables), this will not only
add one more year of service
credit but will add one more
year to your age, so will
reduce the early retirement
reduction

PART 4: SCENARIO PLANNING

Part 4 looks at several different "life scenarios" for PERA members as examples of how you might combine Parts 1 through 3 into a coherent life financial plan, and then gives you a structure to create a personalized scenario for yourself.

4.1: SOME PERA RETIREMENT SCENARIOS

TL;DR: By looking at some different career length and retirement scenarios, you can make decisions along the way that can help you achieve your goals.

The following are some example retirement scenarios for PERA members. While they are not random (I did put some thought into what might be some likely scenarios), they are simply a few examples to illustrate the concept. Please don't feel constrained by them or that one of them must be the "right" scenario for you. Think of them as brainstorming; looking at the possibilities in order to start thinking about what's right for you.

It's also important to realize that, like all long-term projections, these projections will quickly become "off" as actual lived experience deviates from the assumptions involved (and, by necessity, there are lots and lots of assumptions involved). It's best to think of these as **"plausible paths"**, a reasonable outline of paths you might take in order to live the life you want and retire at the age you desire. They aren't meant to be prescriptive, but rather guides to help you make choices and decisions along the way. And, rest assured, you can completely ignore these scenarios and simply learn from - and act upon - the advice in the rest of this book independently of these scenarios.

I envision three different approaches to looking at these scenarios, using the analogy of visiting a model home.

The first approach is akin to driving by the model home but not going inside. You check out the looks of the house from the outside as well as the general neighborhood to see if it might be a good fit for you, but you don't really dive in very deep. So you take a look at the various scenarios below, see which one(s) appeal to you, and then use that information as just general information to help inform some of your financial decisions along the way.

For the second approach you actually stop the car, get out and go inside and take a tour of the model home. You maybe talk a little bit with the salesperson and take home a brochure that talks up the features and the neighborhood and includes a floor plan of the home. For this approach, you go a little bit deeper and try to evaluate which scenario (model home) is the "right" one for you based on your values and your goals. You try to envision yourself "living in the house" and see if it seems right, and you perhaps go so far as to compare your current situation with the details on the spreadsheet and perhaps make some modifications to bring your actual finances closer to the scenario. As time passes, you use the spreadsheet as kind of a scoreboard to see how you are doing and whether you are "ahead" or "behind" your goal.

The final approach is the most intense. Not only do you tour the model home and take home the floor plan, but you get and analyze a copy of the architectural drawings, and perhaps you even meet with the architect to make some changes to the plans before the house is built. Like with the second approach, you compare your current situation with the scenario you've chosen to see how you are doing. But this time you treat the spreadsheet as much more of a blueprint that the builders are actually going to construct from. You make a copy of the spreadsheet and update it with your current financial information and, as time goes by, you continue to update it and then make any necessary adjustments to your financial decisions in order to stay (reasonably) on track for achieving the scenario. This approach is for the real planners out there and for the folks who really like a somewhat prescriptive (or simply detailed) approach.

No matter which approach you take (or some other approach

that I didn't have a good analogy for), I think the scenarios and spreadsheets are worth your time just to see what's possible and what it might take to achieve them. Even if it's just a "drive-by" approach, I think you'll glean some good information from going through them.

You can find detailed spreadsheets to accompany each of the following scenarios at **fischlearning.com/scenarios-for-colorado-public-employees/**.

> **Update December 2021**: The original spreadsheets (below) are too complicated (confusing?) for some folks, so I've created easier, simplified spreadsheets as well in case that is helpful. The original ones (described below) are still available, but you may have a better experience with these simplified spreadsheets.

The scenarios are categorized using three criteria: membership date in PERA, whether you are married or single (and, if married, whether your spouse is also a PERA member), and the possible age you would like to retire (or at least achieve "work optional" status and the ability to stop working in your current PERA-covered job if you so desire). Since the most common public school employee is a teacher, that's the example I'll use, although the scenarios work for any public school PERA member (just the specifics of salary and benefits might be different than what I illustrate).

PERA Membership Date: Your PERA benefits are different depending on when you began PERA employment (and, sometimes, on when you've earned 5 years of service credit). The following scenarios are split into two PERA Membership Date categories, membership date before January 1, 2020 (using HAS Table 7) and membership date after January 1, 2020 (using HAS Table 9). (If your membership date is before 2011, then you actually have slightly better benefits than Table 7, you can find the tables at **copera.org/highest-average-salary-tables**, but to make this digestible in book form we kept it simple).

Marital Status: The scenarios look at three different marital-status variations; a single teacher, a teacher married to another PERA-covered teacher, and a teacher married to a non-PERA covered employee.

Possible Age to Retire: The scenarios look at possibilities of retiring (or at least reaching "work optional" status and being able to stop working at your PERA-covered job) at age 47, 53 and 58. (Again, these were just chosen as possibilities, they are not meant to be prescriptive or your only choices.)

When you look at the permutations of the criteria above, there are a total of 18 different scenarios. We'll look at those 18 permutations through the organizing principle of age of retirement. (And, again, it might not be "retirement", but the time you become "work optional" in your public school job and can decide to do someting else, either volunteer or paid.) By necessity, these scenarios can cover only a small portion of the possible scenarios, so I chose to focus on teachers at the beginning of their teaching career, therefore the spreadsheets and assumptions proceed from an early age. But the process is applicable to you no matter your age, you will simply have to modify the spreadsheets to start with your current age and financial situation.

The following is just a brief description of each scenario, and then you can visit **fischlearning.com/tldr** for much, much more detail.

Retire at Age 47
The first six scenarios lay out a "**plausible path**" for retiring at age 47. As you might suspect, in order to retire at 47 it requires a conscious decision to live within your means and not significantly increase your spending over time. This scenario allows for yearly increases that are typically slightly higher than the assumed rate of inflation (2.5%), but occasionally are slightly lower than that. There are a few years along the way with a slightly larger increase (5-7%). Like all of the scenarios, it assumes that around age 70

your spending stops increasing (health care costs may go up, but other costs typically go down), so spending increases level out and even decline a bit year to year.

Scenario 47-1: Teacher Married to a Teacher, Retire at 47, PERA Membership date **before** January 1, 2020. This example assumes two married 25-year old teachers with Master's degrees, starting their 3rd year of teaching in 2020, with one newborn child. Assume they will complete 15 hours of credit every 3 years to advance on the salary schedule (start at MA + 0, move to MA + 15 after 3 years, then MA + 30 after 6, etc. until maxed out at MA + 90).

Scenario 47-2: Teacher Married to a Teacher, Retire at 47, PERA Membership date **after** January 1, 2020. This example assumes two married 22-year old teachers with Bachelor's degrees, starting their 1st year of teaching in 2020, who have one child at age 25. Assume they will get their Master's degrees by age 25, and then complete 15 hours of credit every 3 years to advance on the salary schedule (move to MA + 15 after 3 years, then MA + 30 after 6, etc. until maxed out at MA + 90)

Scenario 47-3: Teacher Married to Non-PERA Member, Retire at 47, PERA Membership date **before** January 1, 2020. This example assumes a married 25-year old couple, one a teacher with a Master's degree starting their 3rd year of teaching in 2020, the other a non-PERA member with a Social Security covered job, with one newborn child. Assumes the teacher will complete 15 hours of credit every 3 years to advance on the salary schedule (start at MA + 0, move to MA + 15 after 3 years, then MA + 30 after 6, etc. until maxed out at MA + 90).

Scenario 47-4: Teacher Married to Non-PERA Member, Retire at 47, PERA Membership date **after** January 1, 2020. This example assumes married 22-year olds, one a teacher with a Bachelor's degree, starting their 1st year of teaching in 2020, the other a Non-PERA Member who is covered by Social Security, who have one child at age 25. Assume the teacher will get their Master's degrees by age 25, and then complete 15 hours of credit every 3 years to advance on the salary schedule (move to MA + 15 after 3 years, then MA + 30 after 6, etc. until maxed out at MA + 90).

Scenario 47-5: Single Teacher, Retire at 47, PERA Membership date **before** January 1, 2020. This example assumes a single 25-year old teacher with a Master's degree, starting their 3rd year of teaching in 2020. Assume they will complete 15 hours of credit every 3 years to advance on the salary schedule (start at MA + 0, move to MA + 15 after 3 years, then MA + 30 after 6, etc. until maxed out at MA + 90).

Scenario 47-6: Single Teacher, Retire at 47, PERA Membership date **after** January 1, 2020. This example assumes a single 22-year old teacher with a Bachelor's degree, starting their 1st year of teaching in 2020. Assume they will earn a Master's degree by age 25, and then complete 15 hours of credit every 3 years to advance on the salary schedule (start at MA + 0, move to MA + 15 after 3 years, then MA + 30 after 6, etc. until maxed out at MA + 90).

Retire at Age 53

The next six scenarios lay out a **"plausible path"** for retiring at age 53. Compared to the scenario retiring at 47, this scenario gives you a higher income to live on, both while working and when retired. You still have to live within your means, but the initial amounts to live on as well as the yearly increases are larger. Assumes that around age 70 spending stops increasing (health care costs may go up, but other costs go down), so increases level out and even decline a bit year to year.

Scenario 53-1: Teacher Married to a Teacher, Retire at 53, PERA Membership date **before** January 1, 2020. This example assumes two married 25-year old teachers with Master's degrees, starting their 3rd year of teaching in 2020, with one newborn child. Assume they will complete 15 hours of credit every 3 years to advance on the salary schedule (start at MA + 0, move to MA + 15 after 3 years, then MA + 30 after 6, etc. until maxed out at MA + 90).

Scenario 53-2: Teacher Married to a Teacher, Retire at 53, PERA Membership date **after** January 1, 2020. This example assumes two married 22-year old teachers with Bachelor's degrees, starting their 1st year of teaching in 2020, who have one child at age 25. Assume they will get their Master's degrees by age 25, and then complete 15 hours of credit every 3 years to advance on the salary schedule (move to MA + 15 after 3 years, then MA + 30 after 6, etc. until maxed out at MA + 90)

Scenario 53-3: Teacher Married to Non-PERA Member, Retire at 53, PERA Membership date **before** January 1, 2020. This example assumes a married 25-year old couple, one a teacher with a Master's degree starting their 3rd year of teaching in 2020, the other a non-PERA member with a Social Security covered job, with one newborn child. Assumes the teacher will complete 15 hours of credit every 3 years to advance on the salary schedule (start at MA + 0, move to MA + 15 after 3 years, then MA + 30 after 6, etc. until maxed out at MA + 90).

Scenario 53-4: Teacher Married to Non-PERA Member, Retire at 53, PERA Membership date **after** January 1, 2020. This example assumes married 22-year olds, one a teacher with a Bachelor's degree, starting their 1st year of teaching in 2020, the other a Non-PERA Member who is covered by Social Security, who have one child at age 25. Assume the teacher will get their Master's degrees by age 25, and then complete 15 hours of credit every 3 years to advance on the salary schedule (move to MA + 15 after 3 years, then MA + 30 after 6, etc. until maxed out at MA + 90).

Scenario 53-5: Single Teacher, Retire at 53, PERA Membership date **before** January 1, 2020. This example assumes a single 25-year old teacher with a Master's degree, starting their 3rd year of teaching in 2020. Assume they will complete 15 hours of credit every 3 years to advance on the salary schedule (start at MA + 0, move to MA + 15 after 3 years, then MA + 30 after 6, etc. until maxed out at MA + 90).

Scenario 53-6: Single Teacher, Retire at 53, PERA Membership date **after** January 1, 2020. This example assumes a single 22-year old teacher with a Bachelor's degree, starting their 1st year of teaching in 2020. Assume they will earn a Master's degree by age 25, and then complete 15 hours of credit every 3 years to advance on the salary schedule (start at MA + 0, move to MA + 15 after 3 years, then MA + 30 after 6, etc. until maxed out at MA + 90).

Retire at Age 58

The final six scenarios lay out a **"plausible path"** for retiring at age 58. Compared to the scenarios retiring at 47 or 53, this scenario gives you an even higher income to live on, both while working and when retired. You still have to live within your means, but the initial amounts to live on as well as the yearly increases are larger. Assumes that around age 70 spending stops increasing (health care costs may go up, but other costs go down), so increases level out and even decline a bit year to year.

Scenario 58-1: Teacher Married to a Teacher, Retire at 58, PERA Membership date **before** January 1, 2020.

Scenario 58-2: Teacher Married to a Teacher, Retire at 58, PERA Membership date **after** January 1, 2020.

Scenario 58-3: Teacher Married to Non-PERA Member, Retire at 58, PERA Membership date **before** January 1, 2020. This example assumes a married 25-year old couple, one a teacher with a Master's degree starting their 3rd year of teaching in 2020, the other a non-PERA member with a Social Security covered job, with one newborn child. Assumes the teacher will complete 15 hours of credit every 3 years to advance on the salary schedule (start at MA + 0, move to MA + 15 after 3 years, then MA + 30 after 6, etc. until maxed out at MA + 90).

Scenario 58-4: Teacher Married to Non-PERA Member, Retire at 58, PERA Membership date **after** January 1, 2020. This example assumes married 22-year olds, one a teacher with a Bachelor's degree, starting their 1st year of teaching in 2020, the other a Non-PERA Member who is covered by Social Security, who have one child at age 25. Assume the teacher will get their Master's degrees by age 25, and then complete 15 hours of credit every 3 years to advance on the salary schedule (move to MA + 15 after 3 years, then MA + 30 after 6, etc. until maxed out at MA + 90).

Scenario 58-5: Single Teacher, Retire at 58, PERA Membership date **before** January 1, 2020. This example assumes a single 25-year old teacher with a Master's degree, starting their 3rd year of teaching in 2020. Assume they will complete 15 hours of credit every 3 years to advance on the salary schedule (start at MA + 0, move to MA + 15 after 3 years, then MA + 30 after 6, etc. until maxed out at MA + 90).

Scenario 58-6: Single Teacher, Retire at 58, PERA Membership date **after** January 1, 2020. This example assumes a single 22-year old teacher with a Bachelor's degree, starting their 1st year of teaching in 2020. Assume they will earn a Master's degree by age 25, and then complete 15 hours of credit every 3 years to advance on the salary schedule (start at MA + 0, move to MA + 15 after 3 years, then MA + 30 after 6, etc. until maxed out at MA + 90).

Again, you can find additional descriptions of each scenario as well as detailed year-by-year spreadsheets for each at **fischlearning.com/scenarios-for-colorado-public-employees/**.

A Note About Social Security

While PERA is a Social Security replacement system, it's possible that you will qualify for some Social Security as well based on your other, Social Security-covered employment. (You need 10 years of

Social Security earnings to qualify; that might be from work in high school, in college, side hustles during your career or in the summers, or working after retirement from PERA.)

But even if you do have ten years of earnings, the amount you receive will likely be much less than what your Social Security statement indicates, because of the **Windfall Elimination Provision (WEP)**. You can use this online calculator (**ssa.gov/ benefits/retirement/planner/anyPiaWepjs04.html**) to calculate how much your benefit will be reduced. (The WEP can reduce, but not eliminate, your social security benefit.) (See **bit.ly/wepgpo** for more.)

If you have a spouse who receives Social Security, you normally might be eligible to receive a survivor's benefit if they were to predecease you. But the **Government Pension Offset (GPO)** will likely completely eliminate that if you have a decent PERA pension (see **ssa.gov/benefits/retirement/planner/gpo-calc.html**)

Another great resource is **opensocialsecurity.com.**

4.2: CREATE YOUR OWN PERA RETIREMENT SCENARIO

TL;DR: *If you don't like the scenarios I've whipped up, create your own!*

As indicated previously, there are various approaches you can take as the lens through which you view these scenarios. Some of those approaches might include making a copy of the relevant spreadsheet, updating the starting numbers to match your current situation, and then modifying the spreadsheet year by year as time goes by.

But, if you choose, you can also "roll your own" scenario. Simply take the scenario that is closest to what you envision, make a copy of the spreadsheet, and then start modifying it to fit your specific envisioned scenario. For example, maybe you want to retire really early, but after looking at the spreadsheet, just don't think it will be possible for you to do that by age 47. But perhaps it's close enough to what you think is manageable that if you worked 3 more years (to age 50), you think you could do it. In that case, you copy the spreadsheet, then go to the point of divergence (age 48 in this case) and make changes to the rows after that to reflect the additional years you are planning on working. This will involve getting into the formulas embedded in the spreadsheet, but it's not terribly difficult (and I am happy to help you with that process - free of charge - if you reach out).

Or, alternatively, maybe you think the retiring at 58 scenario is closer to what's reasonable for you, but you think you might be a bit "ahead" of that projection and think you could probably do it by age 56. Again, you could copy the spreadsheet, but this time modify the rows starting after age 56 to reflect stopping work and seeing if you can make the numbers work out for a long retirement.

And, in the end, you can just look at all of these scenarios as just informational (the first approach), and simply focus on making good financial decisions based on the information earlier in the book. But, for those of you who want to dive a little deeper, doing some "what if" brainstorming using these scenarios can be very helpful and can illustrate what might be possible for you.

CONCLUSION: SUSTAINABILITY

TL;DR: Sustainability is about more than just the environment, it's about designing your life in such a way that you can live the life you want to live.

"Often when you think you're at the end of something, you're at the beginning of something else." — *Fred Rogers*

The idea of sustainability is most often associated with the environment, but it also applies to your financial life. The whole purpose of this book is to help you get started on a path that allows you to live your best life, the life you want to lead. Inherent in that is the idea of sustainability, the ability to sustain the life that you want to lead.

Hopefully the **very brief introduction** that this book provided to some of the important financial decisions you need to make will get you interested enough to learn more about these issues. You don't have to be an accountant, a Wall Street trader, or a tax expert to make good decisions, you just need a little bit of knowledge and the wisdom to act on that knowledge.

Just a reminder that this was designed for the TL;DR reader, so it didn't explain the reasons why to do each thing or link to the data that backs each assertion ("about 100 pages, about an hour or two"). I even recommended in the introduction that you probably shouldn't buy or read this book, that instead you should spend some time exploring more thorough and in-depth resources. So, while this book gives you a good start and you hopefully found it helpful, if it's sparked your curiosity and you're willing to invest a bit more time to learn more you will achieve even better results. There are many, many, many resources (books, websites, online communities, etc.) available to you, I've tried to curate just a few of them (along with the scenario spreadsheets) at **fischlearning.com/tldr.** Good luck making the financial decisions that will help you lead **your good life.**

❖ ❖ ❖

If you liked this book and found it helpful, please consider leaving a rating or review on Amazon. Please also consider recommending it (or loaning it!) to other Colorado public school teachers. If you are an administrator, superintendent, school board member, or union leader, consider purchasing this book for your new teachers each year. It not only will make a difference in their financial lives, but it will allow them to be even better teachers because they feel confident in their finances.

If you have questions or feedback, or simply want to talk about your financial situation, please reach out to me at **karl@fischlearning.com** or leave feedback at **bit.ly/tldrfeedback** (really, I *like* talking about this stuff)

Learn More

> **fischlearning.com/tldr/**
>
> **fischlearning.com/tldr_resources/**
>
> **fischlearning.com/scenarios-for-colorado-public-employees/**
>
> **Twitter:** @karlfisch **Facebook:** facebook.com/karlfisch/

TL;DR: GETTING STARTED

Spend less than you make and invest the rest in low-cost, diversified index funds with an asset allocation appropriate for your risk tolerance and investment time horizon.

1. **Bank Accounts and Credit Cards (1.5 & 1.6)**: Optimize these and choose the best accounts for your circumstances.

2. **Income (1.14 & 3.1)**: Advance horizontally on the salary schedule as far as you can as quickly as you can.

3. **Investments (1.10-1.13 & 3.2)**: For **all** of your investments (401k, 403b, 457, IRA, HSA, Taxable Brokerage Account), make sure you are not with a high-fee vendor or have high-fee investments. If you do, switch to a low-fee vendor and invest in low-cost, diversified index funds. Also think carefully about both your asset allocation and your risk tolerance and perhaps make adjustments.

4. **Pension (All of Part 2 & 3.1)**: Take the time to figure out if you are eligible to purchase service credit and seriously consider doing that if you are eligible. Also consider earning extra income during your Average Monthly Compensation years.

5. **Retirement Scenarios (4.2)**: Take some time to play around with some of the retirement scenarios just to familiarize yourself with the possibilities. Think carefully about how your pension (PERA) and additional investments (401k/403b/457/IRA/Taxable Brokerage) can add up to help you live your 'good life' in retirement.

6. **Learn More**: Visit **fischlearning.com/tldr_resources/** and **fischlearning.com/scenarios-for-colorado-public-employees/** and explore the resources available there to continue your financial education.

Made in the USA
Las Vegas, NV
20 June 2023

73677535R00066